The Windfall Yachts

A Legacy of Goodwill

ISBN 978-0-9542547-1-1

Published by Topsy II Publishing
PO Box 22
Stoke sub Hamdon
Somerset TA14 6WW

October 2007
1st edition

Printed by Short Run Press Ltd, Exeter.

Contents

Cover photograph by Beken of Cowes:
The 100 square metre Windfall *Wal* (later *Collingwood* then *Wal* next *Merlin*
now *Zeearend*) in the Solent in 1954.

Prince Philip helming *Bloodhound* 1962
Beken of Cowes

FOREWORD

It has long been a custom for victors in war to claim reparations from the defeated enemy, but I very much doubt whether any such reparations have achieved so much social good as the acquisition of the German Navy's sailing yachts.

Countless young service and civilian people were given the opportunity to experience the challenge of offshore racing, and the satisfaction of successfully completing an ocean passage under sail.

I congratulate the author on putting together this comprehensive account of what became known as the 'Windfall Yachts'. It is a story that deserves to be recorded, if only as an example that something really good can come out of the horror of war.

This book is dedicated to the spirit of goodwill
generated by the Windfall yachts.

All proceeds from the sale of this book are in aid of the charity
Seafarers UK (King George's Fund for Sailors)

ACKNOWLEDGEMENTS

It is a great honour that HRH The Duke of Edinburgh has written a foreword. A naval officer, the Duke of course was a keen sailor in earlier years, has been Admiral of the Royal Naval Sailing Association since 1952 and is also President of Seafarers UK (King George's Fund for Sailors), to whom all proceeds are donated.

It has only been possible to produce this book because of all the many individuals and organisations listed below who have selflessly provided material and taken the time and trouble to respond to enquiries. To all of these I am so very grateful. Special thanks must go to Tony Venables and John Kapp, who have both long experience of running a number of Windfalls until recently and also a deep interest in the history of the yachts. They have unfailingly shared material from their particular spheres gathered over many years for which I cannot thank them enough.

Individuals

For many reasons this book has taken an inordinate time to produce. All the following have contributed in various ways, usually in letter, interview or e-mail form. A number have since died, lost contact, risen in rank or left the services. For simplicity therefore ranks (and some were high) and decorations (and there were many) have been omitted as has any reference to 'the late'. This perhaps fits in well as of course in a vessel at sea, men and women are all of one company.

Leo Aarens, Bruce Allen, Terry Andrews, David Angwin, Peter Archer, Christopher Armstrong, Jan Aylen, Michael Barrow, J A Bayley, Katie Binns, Paddy Blagden, Richard Bickford, Dave Bishop, Ron Bond, Fred and Heather Bouter, Peter Broadbent, Clive Brown, Malcolm Brown, Hugh Bruce, Erroll Bruce, David Brunton, John Clark, John Clementson, David Clifton, David Cook, Frank Craig, Philip Crampton, C G Crill, Guy Crowden, John Croydon. John Davies, Simon Davies, Christopher Dean, Graham de-Chair, David Dickenson, Barry Eastley, John Eddie, Bjarne Engen, Michael English, Baz Ennels, Chris Esplin-Jones, Merryn Fairbank, Lloyd Foster, D E French, Norman Fitzgerald, Ernest Le Flufy, Robert Franks, F G Fray, Patrick Fryer, Richard Garlick, Michael Gill, Jack Glennie, Patrick Glennie, Robin Graham, John Goslin, Janet Grieve, Richard Hawkins, Roy Hawkes, C H Hayward, K J Hazard, Richard Hewitt, Martin Hayden, George Hogg, Paul & Lorraine Holmes, Guy Hornet, John Hunt, Phil Hutchins, Jimmy James, Reggy Jeffes, Mike Jones, John Kapp, Mr Keneway, Klaus Kinast, Derek Kitch, Robert Knocker, Graham Laslett, H

Lawrence, Don MacGregor, Jimmy Mackworth, Nigel Malim, Mr McKenzie-Smith, John McLennan, Ted Mellor, David Miller, Gordon Moey, Lord David Mottistone, Robin McNish, Tim Norman-Walker, Roland Notley, John Milne, Tony Naish, Hugh Owen, Graham Pass, Nigel Pearson, John Peddie, Robbie Perrin, Loftus Peyton-Jones, Freddie Phillips, Bill Pillar, John Regnard, Christela Rezek-Clark, Peter Richardson, Robin Richardson, Rupert Richardson, Tony Ricketts, Karen Roach, Frank Robertshaw, Patrick Rowe, Paddy Ryan, Hans Schaedla, Otto Schlenzka, Morin Scott, Jess Simpson-Gee, Eoin Sloan, Ewen Southby-Tailyour, Richard Spalding, Peter Stapleford, John Stewart, David Stockley-Martin, Peter Thomas, Mike Tremlett, Ron Valent, Tony Vasey, Tony Venables, Humphrey Wallis, C J Ware, James Weir, John Wells, Bill Wynn-Werminck, John West, Jill Westropp, Peter Whelan, A Williams, Charles Williams, John Willis, Peter Willis, Hugh Wilson, Mr Winridge, Raymond Winter, Michael Wise, Eve Woodyear, Peter Wykeham-Martin, CJC Wynne-Edwards.

Organisations

Without fail, when visiting or making contact with the following organisations I have been met with great courtesy, interest and a real wish to help, despite in some cases having an apparent lack of material. Collectively however they have all supplied pieces of the jigsaw (with many still missing) which have contributed to the whole. In alphabetical order:

Abeking & Rasmussen
Aeroplane magazine
Army Sailing Association
Associated Newspapers Limited
Association for Square Metre Yachts
Association of Service Yacht Clubs
Association of Square Metre Yacht Clubs
Beken of Cowes
Britannia Royal Naval College Library
Buckingham Palace Archives
British Kiel Yacht Club
Classic Boat magazine
English Heritage Calshot Castle
Guards Magazine
Household Division Yacht Club
Imperial War Museum
Imperial War Museum Duxford
Kiel Maritime Museum
Kiel Town Museum
Kiel Training Centre
Kieler Yacht Club
Motor Boat and Yachting magazine

National Archives Kew
National Maritime Museum Greenwich
National Maritime Museum Cornwall
Offshore Cruising Club
Portsmouth Studies Library
Royal Air Force Cranwell Library
Royal Air Force Historical Branch
Royal Air Force Museum
Royal Air Force Yacht Club
Royal Artillery Yacht Club
Royal Engineer Yacht Club
Royal Military Academy Sandhurst Library
Royal Naval Engineering College Library
Royal Naval Historical Branch
Royal Naval Museum
Royal Naval Sailing Association
Royal Ocean Racing Club
Royal Signals Yacht Club
Schleswig Town Museum
Sea Scamp Syndicate
Seafarers UK
Southampton Studies Library
The Times Archive
Winchester Local Studies Library

Above all, very special thanks are due to my wife and family, whose patience and encouragement over many years have contributed so much in finally seeing the project through.

The new German 100 square metre yacht FLAMINGO off Kiel in 1936

INTRODUCTION

Cowes Week

*The Admiral, who was not one to whom one
offered unasked for advice,
jumped aboard, brushed me off the wheel
and ordered the anchor to be raised.
Then, finding the wind to be non existent and the tide strong
commanded "Start the engine".
MARABU, in common with virtually all Windfalls,
had no engine*

Lt Cdr JMA Fairbank MVO RN
Queen's Sailing Master 1963–66

This is an unusual story, unique in our maritime history and not told before. It is about a large fleet of ex German yachts mainly built in the 1930s and taken over by the occupying forces in 1945. Many were then sailed to England and formed the core of post war services offshore sailing before branching out into a wider outside world. The yachts were appropriately called Windfalls, a name which continues to this day. A surprising number are still sailing, as classic boats. More are languishing under covers while just a few have known graves. Others have simply disappeared.

To the author, like so many having started offshore sailing in Windfalls and also with an interest in maritime history, it seemed an appropriate subject to research. There would be plenty of records and it should not be too difficult. Having a maritime background in the Royal Navy here was a chance to put something back, for charity.

It was not to be that simple. Like peeling an onion, there was always another layer to go. The National Maritime Museum had no records, nor did the Royal Naval Historical Branch and many other major archives. The one formal Windfall file in the Royal Air Force Historical branch was recorded as being destroyed in the 1950s, not selected for the National Archive. And so it went on: increasingly it became clear that here was a gap in our maritime historical records: part of our nautical heritage. The concept of a book thus evolved: but what sort of book?

Initial thoughts were that it should be a serious academic book, to include highly technical aspects of the yachts for posterity. Another view, advised by a professional author with an eye to mass circulation, was that there must be a woman in it as a continuity character throughout. It is neither of these.

Talking to many ex and current Windfall sailors, there was clearly a need to record the background of the yachts, their history over the years and as far as possible where they are today. Ideally there should be good photographs, although this would not always be possible with some pictures taken 70 years ago in a moving yacht. Personal accounts of yacht collection from Germany should be included to provide the personal touch. There should be a thread of humour throughout, to reflect the sheer enjoyment of sailing these fine yachts. And so the book structure was developed, to be a readable source of reference about the Windfall fleet, to be dipped into at will.

Following advertising for material, letters came in from all over the world, often providing first hand accounts of Windfall activities right back to their collection from Germany. The Royal Naval Sailing Association (RNSA) found files marked Windfalls with letters back to 1945. Similarly the National Archives produced early correspondence from Germany. Records from the colleges, museums and units of the three services have borne fruit while in more recent years e-mails have proved a speedy and invaluable means of communication. Websites have added to the information flow but as with genealogy, website information in itself is not always reliable (sometimes it is wildly inaccurate, but giving apparent authenticity simply by appearing in print) and it has always been necessary to get verification from other sources.

From these responses it was quite clearly apparent that there is a deep affection for the Windfalls, particularly from those who sailed them home or in Europe after the war. After surviving the hazards of war, collecting yachts from Germany, albeit poorly equipped and without engines, was an experience never to be forgotten and many lifelong friendships were formed. Since the war many thousands have been introduced to offshore sailing via the Windfalls who would otherwise not have been. This book recognises all of these and in respect to them all proceeds from it are in aid of Seafarers UK, King George's Fund for Sailors.

An increasing pleasure in this project has been in meeting current owners of Windfalls, who share a common outlook. It is apparent that there is an ingrained sense of history in them all and they regard themselves as temporary guardians, in exactly the same way as those who own or have responsibility for an old building, be it a house or church. Their charge will outlive them and they will do their bit before passing on the baton. As with a building, there will be ups and downs in the life of a Windfall but for every pause in their condition there is usually an upswing later. Like classic cars in a down and out phase, suddenly there is a realisation that despite their distress they must not be scrapped but held in abeyance until better times.

A further pleasure has been in researching in Germany and meeting German sailors including some who sailed Windfalls in younger days. As in other parts of the Continent there is a deep love of wooden boats to be found and the Windfalls still have a special place. The very process of discussing the yachts in Germany with such enjoyment today, some sixty years after their transfer to British hands, is in itself a legacy of goodwill.

Then there has been the pleasure crawling over the yachts and re-living old times. From a distance when seen in a cradle the lines of a 100, 50 and 30 square metre (sq m) Windfall are remarkably similar but how very different they are close to. To squeeze into the fore peak of a 30 sq m is very different to walking into that of a 100 sq m. To stand in the cabin of a 50 sq m, holding on to the handrails on each side reminds one how narrow they are despite their 42 foot length. They are no wider than a 28 foot Twister and how very much safer down below when in a seaway than in a modern wide yacht. Of course Windfalls of today are immensely drier than of old, with better sealants, effectively stopping those annoying drips from the deckhead.

There is a considerable amount of mythology about the Windfall fleet. All the following statements have appeared in print. "The Royal Navy sailed all the yachts to UK". They didn't. "The Royal Air Force sailed all the yachts to UK". They didn't. "WAL (MERLIN) was Hitler's private yacht". She wasn't. "I remember MARABU: she was found under a haystack" She wasn't. "There were about twenty Windfalls". In fact there were over a hundred Windfall yachts and also very many other smaller craft. There are myths to be corrected.

The Windfalls came at a time of national austerity. They contributed greatly to many people's lives, providing training, adventure, companionship, recreation and sheer fun. All positives at a difficult time, which deserve to be recorded.

For these various reasons, there is a story to be told. Here then is a book, part history, part reference and part anthology, about the British Windfall fleet, sourced from original material rather than myths. As with all research there will be more to add but it is offered as a start to record this important missing niche in our maritime heritage.

M.C.

MAP OF SOUTH BALTIC

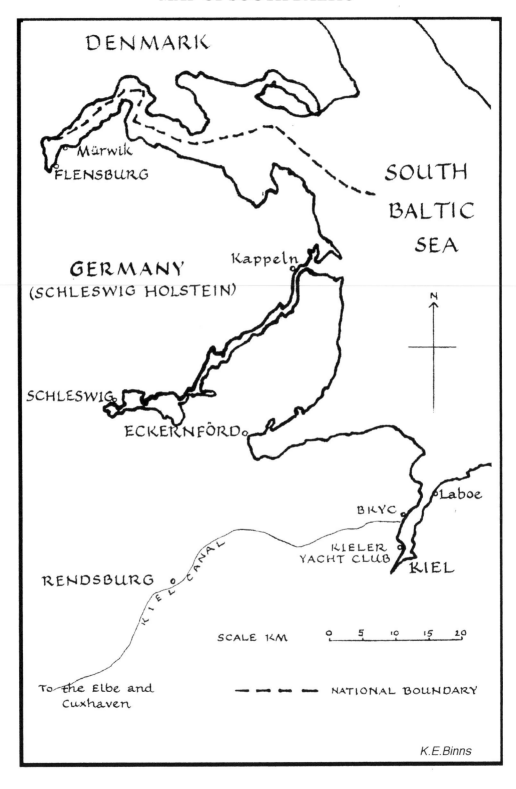

DENMARK

Mürwik
FLENSBURG

SOUTH
BALTIC
SEA

GERMANY
(SCHLESWIG HOLSTEIN)

Kappeln

N

SCHLESWIG

ECKERNFÖRD

Laboe

BRYC

KIELER
YACHT CLUB

KIEL

RENDSBURG

KIEL CANAL

SCALE KM   0   5   10   15   20

To the Elbe and
Cuxhaven

— — — NATIONAL BOUNDARY

K.E.Binns

CHAPTER 1. HISTORICAL

WHY THE WINDFALLS WERE BUILT

The Windfall story really began in 1919 when the Versailles Treaty was signed, limiting the size of the German armed forces. Strict limits were placed on the size and number of warships permitted to be built, together with manpower restrictions while all German naval and military air activities were banned. In practice various loopholes were developed to get round these constraints and by 1932 a large ship and aircraft build programme was commenced. This in turn led to a massive expansion of manpower and the need for more training facilities.

Admiral Erich Raeder
Imperial War Museum

The German Navy (Kriegsmarine), under Admiral Raeder, had always placed great store on the value of sailing to develop basic seamanship, self reliance and an understanding of the sea. It was natural therefore, with the great manpower expansion under way, that the Navy's existing fleet of training yachts needed to be expanded and between 1935 and 1939 large orders were placed by the Kriegsmarine with the major boat building yards. Additionally hundreds of additional inshore boats and dinghies were built for basic boat handling training. With war looming these yacht and small craft orders must have been manna from heaven for the yacht building firms, many of whom had traditional roots going back to the turn of the century.

In parallel with this in 1935 the restrictions imposed by the Versailles Treaty were largely lifted. Before 1935 German military aviation was controlled by the Navy and the Army and it was not until that year that the existence of a separate German Air Force (Luftwaffe) was proclaimed. Meanwhile a fleet of gliders was built for airmanship training, on the lines of the yachts for the Navy's seamanship training.

German glider of the 1930s

It was not long before a requirement also arose for yachts for the Luftwaffe. At its head was a most dynamic figure, Air Marshall Herman Goering, soon to be Deputy to Hitler who considered that all aviation matters should come under him and there were disputes between him and Admiral Raeder. An additional complication was introduced when by the mid 1930s an aircraft carrier programme was established and the first ship, KMS GRAF ZEPPELIN laid down which was to have an effect on the expanding aircrew training programme. Because of these major changes in aviation requirements a considerable number of German naval officers were transferred to the Luftwaffe. Otto Schlenzka, the present Commodore (Admiral in British terms) of the Kieler Yacht Club, who

Air Marshall Goering visiting unknown yacht

joined the German Navy in 1936, remembers at the Naval Academy in his year alone a complete "Crew" (or Term) of cadets being transferred to the Luftwaffe as a batch. They were trained at the island of Rueden, and their facilities included the use of yachts based there, for navigational and seamanship training. And so it was that in addition to the naval yacht orders a number were ordered by the Reichsluftfahrtministerium (RLM) the Reich Air Ministry, including several larger yachts.

It has been said that a number of the larger Kriegsmarine and Luftwaffe yachts were built for the use of senior military officers and their families. There is no particular evidence of this. While Admiral Raeder was a sailor, certainly Air Marshall Goering was not and it is more likely that the yachts were built for training but also used for occasional recreation including by senior officers.

In any event by 1939 there existed in the German services a large fleet of high quality yachts, mostly new, being used by Naval and some Luftwaffe officers.

THE WAR YEARS

During the war the yachts were mainly laid up in the southern Baltic around the Kiel, Schleswig and Cuxhaven areas. Some were damaged or lost through bombing but of the large fleet remaining most were generally in good condition at the end of the war. Of course the sails and running rigging had deteriorated in the war years but the well built hulls, masts and fittings were a credit to their builders and were to last for many years, some to this day.

REPARATIONS

The fleet, all of which was government owned, was taken as part of the post war reparations, about a third going to Russia, a few to America but the majority to the British Forces. This term Reparations, a World War I term, more popularly but wrongly described as Spoils of War (which rather implies an illegal process for personal gain), is a legal post war procedure for the transfer of equipment or facilities from government to government after a war. Looting is another matter altogether, which is a totally illegal and reprehensible action. In earlier centuries prizes of war were very much part of naval life and surrendered enemy warships were often immediately put into use under the captor's flag. In more modern times a number of ex German ocean liners were taken over and put into service under a new name: for example the Cunard White Star Line liner MAJESTIC was formerly the German BISMARK before the first world war. While she was privately owned, she like others in the two world wars was taken as a reparation as part replacement for British ocean liners sunk during the war years. Reparations could equally apply to warships, aircraft, ocean liners, yachts or any other moveable items. In the case of the yacht fleet, there were no German services to use them after the war and it was perfectly correct that they were to be put to very good use by the Allies. The yachts became known as Windfalls.

THE TERM WINDFALL

The first known formally recorded use of the term Windfall may be found in the official Report of Proceedings to the Commander in Chief Portsmouth, the Senior Naval Officer Schleswig Holstein and others on 27 May 1946 by Commander I.G. Aylen Royal Navy following his delivery trip of the 60 ton German yacht NORDWIND to UK. Commenting on the future of NORDWIND and another large yacht SKAGERRAK, he states "Without any question these two yachts (and the similar OSTWIND, which is already being commissioned by the U.S. Navy) are a WINDFALL to the nation, which cannot be repeated". This report also went to the Royal Naval Sailing Association (RNSA). Commander Aylen had been a leading light in services sailing in the Kiel area since he arrived there as the war ended in early May 1945 and during that year skippered NORDWIND.

As more and more German yachts were sailed to England in 1946 the administration of them caused increasing problems. The RNSA acted as an adviser to the Admiralty and the Association of Service Yacht Clubs (the newly formed delegated authority for recommending allocation of the German yachts assigned to the services) but did not have any direct authority. Nevertheless the RNSA was bombarded with queries from all sides, involving many meetings. It is generally recognised that at yet another RNSA meeting about the yachts in early 1946 that the name "Admiralty Windfall" emerged and thereafter used officially as just "Windfall", a simple and effective name. It is reasonable, in view of Commander Aylen's close links with the RNSA and his early reference of "a windfall to the nation" in his report, that he may be considered the originator of the term. There are those who say that the name was used in Germany in 1945 but no record has been found confirming that, certainly not officially. Specifically in 1946 Admiralty correspondence the yacht ORION was described as a Windfall and since that time the term has been officially used to this day. The dictionary definitions "An unexpected legacy" and "Something blown down by the wind" would certainly seem apt.

Commander Jan Aylen aboard Nordwind

When the Britannia Royal Naval College 50 sq m Windfalls were eventually replaced by newly built yachts in 1959, the Admiralty instructed that the term "Windfall" was to be dropped in favour of "Seamanship Training Craft". This was done for these and subsequent new craft, which of course were not Windfalls, but the ex-German yachts continued to be officially so named and have continued to be so throughout the world to this day some 60 years later.

So what is a Windfall? There can be many interpretations but it is generally accepted that a Windfall is an ex German government owned yacht which was acquired by the British occupying forces in Germany and sailed by the services in Germany, UK and the Commonwealth. While this is a bit of a mouthful it is important to understand the definition. Many German craft of all sorts were taken as reparations, including large sailing ships, warships and ocean liners: other nations, particularly Russia and the United States, had their share. The term Windfall is British, referring only to sailing vessels and in particular, yachts.

In time of course the services gradually disposed of them into civilian ownership where to this day they are still termed Windfalls.

Having said this, there are one or two loopholes. Some German yachts acquired in 1945 and sailed in the Baltic by the occupying forces were in fact privately owned. In general the owners were only too happy about this, as it ensured their safe keeping and maintenance at that difficult post war period. In due course the yachts were all returned to their German owners and in most cases their use paid for. These yachts, sailed as they were by the occupying forces, could reasonably be called Windfalls and are therefore included here.

Very many small craft were taken as reparations and both used widely in Europe and all over the Commonwealth. Most of these Stars, Sharpies and Olympics were in fact given names and some would argue that they should be designated Windfalls, particularly as they were listed in the Admiralty documentation along with the yachts. Although technically they were indeed Windfalls, other than in these early lists they were never described as such but are mentioned here to complete the overall picture. In practice in all subsequent official correspondence the term Windfall was only used for yachts.

GERMAN PRE WAR SAILING

Kaiserlichen Yacht Club 1926

The Baltic has always been a delightful area in which to sail, with virtually no tides, good offshore stretches and thousands of islands to explore and provide shelter. At the same time it has its share of strong winds, currents and depth changes due to tidal surges, providing plenty of challenges. The countries surrounding the Baltic have a long maritime tradition and the Kiel area was a natural place for Germany to use as a base. Also before 1895 the Eider Canals gave access to the North Sea but only for relatively small craft and when Kaiser Wilhelm Canal (the Kiel Canal) was opened in that year it provided a very much larger and more direct link.

Germany has a strong yacht racing tradition, really starting in 1882 when a group of officers of the Imperial German Navy held a regatta at Kiel which rapidly became a popular annual event. In 1887 the group, with 112 members, formed itself into a formal organisation known as Marine-Regatta-Verein (MRV) "for the sole purpose of promoting the joy of sailing" although in practice the MRV was primarily concerned with yacht racing. The joint Chairmen were Vice Admiral von Blanc and Marine Engineer Busley and it was in that year that the MRV founded a yacht club at Kiel, known initially as Marine Regattaverein in the very premises that are now the Kieler Yacht Club. By 1891 the club had 500 members and to give the club more stature Kaiser Wilhelm II was invited to be Commodore which he readily accepted. From then on the club was named Kaiserlichen (or "Imperial") Yacht Club, later becoming the Kieler Yacht Club. Also in 1891 the Kaiser bought the THISTLE, the British challenger for the America's Cup. Renamed the METEOR, she was brought to Kiel which from then on became the focus of German yachting. A new METEOR was then built and the old one re-christened COMET, used as a training yacht for yacht hands in the Baltic. The Kaiser became a regular sailor at Cowes and other British ports, together with Prince Henry of Prussia, who owned IRENE. They sailed against the Prince of Wales in BRITANNIA and other well known yachtsmen in SATANITA, VALKYRIE, IVERNA, CALLUNA and others. As the years went on the Kaiser was to have successive METEORs built. For the first three he employed British skippers and mainly British crews but having gained experience switched to an all German crew in METEOR IV, a 400 ton schooner launched in 1909.

Kiel Regatta 1936. Seeotter in the foreground

By 1914 Kiel Week had become second only to Cowes in the yachting racing and social calendar. After a post war lull there was a surge in activity in the 1920s and by the early 1930s there were over 300 sailing clubs in Germany. With its excellent facilities Kiel was an automatic choice of venue for the sailing events in the 1936 Olympic Games in which Germany won the Star Class out of the four classes. By 1938, with 3600 members, the Marine Regatta-Verein claimed to be the largest yacht club in Europe.

In the German services there was a tradition of training under sail. Sea training for midshipmen was carried out in large three masted sail training ships such as HORST WESSEL and ALBERT LEO SCHLAGETER, each carrying 200 midshipmen, with smaller yachts for coastal navigational training. Then in the mid 1930's as we have seen there was a massive yacht building programme to provide high quality yachts for seamanship and navigational training both for the Kriegsmarine (Navy) and the Luftwaffe (Air Force). All the major boat builders were set to work and this fleet, principally of 50 square metre (loa 42 ft) and 100 square metre (loa 55 ft) yachts, was built.

By the mid 1930's an Annual International Naval Regatta had developed at Kiel, with serving naval crews from Denmark, England, Estonia, France, Germany, Holland, Italy, Poland, Romania, Sweden, and Turkey, sailing the Star Class dinghies for various prizes the premier one being the "Hindenburg Cup". This was keenly contested on the water with considerable national pride at stake. A feature of these events was the tremendous hospitality of the German hosts and the great goodwill which developed between the teams. The 1938 event was won by Germany (with Italy second and England third). The RN team leader was Captain Baillie-Grohman, Chairman of the RNSA and who in 1945 would be Senior Naval Officer Schleswig Holstein as a Rear Admiral and a leading figure in the Windfall story at that time. One English

LEADERS OF THE TEAMS.
Left to right: Holland, Poland, Sweden, England, Germany, Admiral Goetting, Roumania, Denmark, Turkey, Italy, France, Esthonia.

Team Leaders of the 1938 Naval Regatta at Kiel

100 sq m Flamingo.
Sailing in the Kiel area 1936

helmsman, Sub Lieutenant Woodcock, was outstanding and he returned as team captain for the 5th and last regatta in 1939 to take the Hindenburg Trophy home for the Royal Navy. Poignantly only two years later in the war Lieutenant Woodcock was lost in HMS BARHAM and his father later set up a Woodcock Trust in his memory towards the cost of financing RNSA high performance dinghies. This trust still exists as does the Hindenburg Cup which is competed for at Dartmouth to this day, a legacy of those tremendously successful pre war naval regattas at Kiel.

While the naval regattas were held at Kiel, the visiting naval parties were taken round the area including to the German Naval Officers' college at Murwick, near Flensburg some sixty miles to the north. It was there that the German 30 and 50 square metre yachts could be seen on a daily basis being sailed in and out of the yacht basin by the midshipmen. None of the yachts had engines. To quote from the report on the 1938 regatta, "What appealed to us more than anything else was a large yacht harbour containing over a hundred craft from 50 square metre yachts to Olympic Monotypes all provided by the German Admiralty for the use and instruction of midshipmen. No wonder the German Naval Officer is such a good helmsman. We arrived just as a race was finishing and I think that we were all impressed by the quiet and seamanlike way these lads sailed 50 and 30 square metres into the basins and into the rather closely packed pens."

Meanwhile the German offshore services sailing challenge progressed, with increasingly successful results in the Baltic and also in the Royal Ocean Racing Club programme. The first recorded entrant of a future Windfall in these races was ASTA, an 85 foot yawl entered by the German Navy and took first place out of twelve in the 1934 Heligoland to Copenhagen Race. In 1935 she again sailed for the German Navy but in later years was entered by the Marine Regatta Verein. She raced again less successfully in the same race in 1935 and further races in later years including the 1937 Fastnet Race.

A significant entrant for the 1937 Heligoland Race was PELIKAN, the first 100 square metre yacht entrant. This class was to become the largest of the true Windfall yachts retained by the British services after the war, the larger yachts being disposed of within a few years. She was renamed OVERLORD, initially of the Royal Engineer Yacht Club and one of the few 100 sq m yachts still sailing today. The star pre war racing yacht in the fleet, only completed in 1939, was the 300 square metre NORDWIND, sailing for the German Navy (Kriegsmarine). She took line honours in the Fastnet Race of that year in a time that was not beaten for 26 years.

Thus before the war there was a strong offshore sailing tradition in Germany, principally in the early 1930s with both government and privately owned yachts. The building of a large new yacht fleet by the government accelerated this tradition and the German services increasingly started to make themselves felt before the war brought all offshore sailing to a halt.

BRITISH PRE WAR SERVICES OFFSHORE SAILING

In the wealthy civilian world of yacht sailing of the 19th and early 20th centuries Britain led the way in Europe (the America's Cup excepting). The Royal Yacht Squadron, formed in 1815, was the focal point and Cowes the premier regatta. By 1925 the Royal Ocean Racing Club was established to organise offshore racing for the growing fleets of smaller craft.

In the British services however there was relatively little experience of offshore sailing other than in privately owned yachts. The Royal Naval College at Dartmouth had AMARYLLIS, privately owned and on loan and she was entered in four Fastnet Races between 1928 to 1931, always finishing but with little success. A group of naval officers had a yacht TAI MO SHAN built in the Far East, sailed her home and persuaded the Admiralty to buy her for the use of naval cadets. She too was usually at the back of the fleet. The Royal Naval Engineering College at Plymouth had two small yachts TOPSY and TURVY for local sailing and only in 1938 acquired a cruising yacht GAUNTLET 'on loan from the Admiralty'. Most naval seamanship training was done in open service boats such as the cutters and whalers as carried in large warships. Unlike many countries Britain did not have large sail training vessels for cadet sea training. While there was the occasional naval officer with his privately owned yacht, offshore sailing by naval officers was in those days more usually undertaken as crew members of civilian yachts. By far the most successful pre war Royal Naval offshore sailor was Lt Commander J Illingworth in his MAID OF MALHAM, who finished third in the 1937 Fastnet Race and had other successes. He was to have many more after the war as one of Britain's leading offshore sailors.

In fact the Army had more (privately owned or in syndicates) offshore yachts than the Navy and in particular the Royal Engineers had a very strong yachting tradition, the Royal Engineer Yacht Club (REYC) being a particularly early British club, established in 1846. The club entered for the first Fastnet Race in 1925, won the second race in 1926 in their yacht ILEX and has competed in every one since – the only club, civilian or service, to do so. The Royal Air Force Yacht Club was inaugurated at Calshot in 1932, entering their yacht EMERLINE in the 1935 Fastnet Race, the year that the Royal Naval Sailing Association was formed.

Thus when the large numbers of Windfalls were taken over in 1945 they were to have a massive and far reaching impact on British services sailing. Suddenly, from having virtually no yachts, they appeared in abundance, not privately owned but owned by the services themselves. And so for the first time the door, which was never to close, was opened wide to all.

CHAPTER 2. The Yachts and Builders

The Square Metre Classes

Although initially after the war the Windfall fleet included a number of miscellaneous yachts, by 1950 the majority of the yachts were of square metre (sq m) classes, usually 100 sq m, 50 sq m and 30 sq m. When listed in the builders records or in Lloyd's Register of Yachts they were simply as 100 sq m etc. It was a definition, i.e. a true class and did not need the string of other measurements and tonnage listed for other yachts.

Behind such a simple definition lay a complicated history. It was in 1905 that the Swedish Yacht Racing Association was formed and proposals forwarded for the adoption of International Yacht Racing Union design formula. In the subsequent years the Royal Swedish Yacht Club adopted a square metre rule for yachts from 22 to 150 sq m, based on maximum sail area together with certain measurements. Therefore before the 1930s there were large numbers of yachts in the Baltic based on a Swedish square metre design.

By the early 1930s the Swedish square metre designs had become so refined for pure racing that some were both uncomfortable and expensive to build and maintain. By then the term "narrow gutted lead mine" had been coined, when narrow yachts were produced with a keel weighing up to 75 per cent of the total displacement. And so it was that in the early 1930s a German square metre class concept was developed to provide for both racing and cruising. A range of one design classes was evolved which would include not only a maximum sail area, mast height, Length Waterline (LWL), fore and aft overhangs and draught. Important additional requirements were added to ensure that the yachts could be lived in, including a minimum beam and freeboard, together with certain accommodation details specifying the number of berths, minimum headroom and cabin floor width. Overall construction to be to a special German Lloyds class standard under the rules of measurement known as the "Seefahrtkreuzer – Klassen". All the classes had one thing in common – they had very beautiful lines, both below

50 sq m hull

Planet. Described wrongly as a 60 sq m

and above the water. The 30 sq m, 50 sq m and 100 sq m yachts were remarkably similar in shape, albeit of radically different size.

There are some who believe that the German square metre classes were based on the Swedish yachts, while others maintain that they were quite independent. Perhaps the answer is somewhere between the two, but the fact is that the German square metre classes did provide a range of cruiser racer yachts that were standardised and while of very high quality were cheaper to maintain than those yachts built exclusively to win races. And so it was that when the requirement arose in the mid 1930s for a yacht fleet of cruiser racer yachts to be built for the German government the German square metre classes were a natural choice.

To complicate the square metre position further, when the Admiralty and other lists of reparations were drawn up in 1945 and 1946, for simplicity the yachts were often described in square metre terms as an indication of size. Thus NIMROD was described as 39 sq m yacht, PLANET as a 60 sq m, GALAHAD as an 85 sq m etc when in practice these classifications were technically incorrect. They often emanated from the original lists provided from Kiel and are only described in that way in the Appendices here for consistency as part of the Windfall history.

It must be remembered that yachts, like houses, can change considerably over the decades, particularly internally and the Windfalls were no exception. Some are unrecognisable internally today compared to their build standard. Also one builder may build to a class but in detail quite differently from another. Originally the 100 sq m, 50 sq m and 30 sq m yachts had six, four and two berths respectively. In due course this rose to usually ten (or even 12 in ROBBE's case), six and four. Most noticeably externally the naval 100 sq m yachts MARABU and MERLIN had sizeable coach roofs fitted before they did Atlantic trips and later FLAMINGO followed suit. RMA Sandhurst's 100 sq m ROBBE also fitted a small and rather unattractive one in her winter 1955 refit and later MARABU and GLADEYE were radically changed by their conversion to ketch rig. Metal masts crept in over the years because they were cheaper and stronger. Later still, in civilian hands, a few hulls have been totally epoxy coated.

The Yachts

There were five types of yachts that were to become known as Windfalls after the war:

1. **Extra Large Cruising Yachts.** These ranged from 125 to 300 square metres (sq m) and may be seen included in Appendix 4. There were a number of these in

Skagerrak. 60 ton yawl
Beken of Cowes

the south Baltic, shown in Chapter 3. While some were ex German government owned (and sailed back to the UK in 1946) a number were privately owned and requisitioned for the use of the occupying forces in Germany immediately after the war and eventually returned to their German owners. With their very high value, maintenance costs and deep draft they were not really suitable for service use and the finest extra large yachts were disposed of and were not used by the British forces in the UK. One or two large old yachts were retained for a short period.

2. **100 Square Metre Yachts.** These were (and most still are) very fine well built yachts of about 25 tons and 55 feet length overall (loa), with up to twelve berths. Their construction was usually mahogany on alternate oak and steel frames, with pine decking. Most of this class were built by the highly respected boat yards Aberking & Rasmussen and Burmester. Ten of these yachts became Windfalls including KONIGIN which was only sailed in Germany for a year before being given back to a private owner. They are listed at Appendix 1. All were Bermudan rig such as AVALANCHE (ex STORCH) opposite but as mentioned above GLADEYE (ex REIHER) and MARABU were later ketch rigged. They were the largest true Windfalls and gave sterling service over many years, sailing in Class 1 races and used for seamanship and adventure training from bases both in UK and the Baltic. Several crossed the Atlantic, sailed in many Tall Ships Races and in more recent years in private hands are still to be seen at home and in the Mediterranean.

While a number are currently laid up, three are sailing regularly today: OVERLORD (ex PELIKAN) based in England, FLAMINGO in Germany still used for services sail training and ZEEAREND (ex WAL then MERLIN) in Holland.

GLADEYE BRIDE

"I crewed the 100 sq m GLADEYE in the first Cowes Week (1947) when she was first in British waters. She lost her mast on the Monday morning before the start of the first day's racing just off the Squadron. Once the mast was gone there was no question of a replacement in those immediate post war days, so the crew dispersed. I went to a cocktail party where I met my wife to be, so some good came out of that debacle". Scots Guards Officer.

100 sq m Windfall Avalanche (ex Storch)
Beken of Cowes

3. 50 Square Metre Yachts. These formed the backbone of Windfall sailing in the British services and are listed at Appendix 2. Weighing 10 tons and with an loa of 42 feet and later with six berths, they were ideal both for offshore class racing and seamanship training. Built of mahogany on oak frames with pine decking,

50 sq m Sea Wraith (ex Seegeist)
Beken of Cowes

they were fine yachts and a number are still in use after 70 years. About forty were sailed back to UK and distributed to the services. They were particularly suited to the establishments and clubs of the three services in the Solent area and at the Royal Naval College Dartmouth, who were allocated six. The Solent service clubs quickly started 50 sq m class racing and the Dartmouth Regatta attracted considerable numbers from the east. All around the UK coast 50 sq m yachts were to be found, allocated to isolated service areas. Together with the 100 sq m Windfalls they were the principal service entrants in the Royal Ocean Racing Club offshore races and put up very creditable performances in the early post war years.

4. Miscellaneous Windfall Yachts. Most of these were quite old and were soon disposed of after the war. The largest was the 85 foot steel auxiliary schooner DUHNEN, built in 1912, while a number of others were built before 1930. There remained a number, many similar in size to 50 sq m and a few to 100 sq m, and were true Windfalls but not built to their class measurements. They were usually described in the builders' records as 'Hochseeyacht' meaning high seas yacht. One such was CAPELLA (ex BORKUM), rated as a 90 sq m. GALAHAD (ex ADLER) was not a 100 sq m as first described, but in fact nearer 85 sq m. PICKLE (ex HELGOLAND), was a 30 ton yawl similar to but slightly larger than the 100 sq m class. Opinions vary about HARPY, one of the Royal Naval College Dartmouth Windfalls, described as a 50 sq m on delivery in 1946 and for some years thereafter but in fact she was slightly different from the others with a higher freeboard and had a different racing rating. By 1956 she was officially described (wrongly) as a 60 sq m. There is a view that in fact, because of her sail area, she was a 50 sq m. She was built by K Vertens, not one of the major 50 sq m builders, and she therefore could have been built slightly differently from those from the traditional yards. The miscellaneous yachts are listed in Appendix 4.

90 sq m Capella (ex Borkum)
Beken of Cowes

5. 30 Square Metre Yachts. While true Windfalls, these were generally too small (at 7 tons and 32 feet loa with up to four berths) for true offshore racing and were somewhat limited for adventure training. They are listed in Appendix 3. In

30 sq m Phoenix (ex Bukanier)

UK they were to be found principally in the Solent area for inshore use. About 20 were brought over from Germany mostly in the ship PLUTO. Many were left in the Baltic, a particularly suitable area for this class, while a number were used very successfully in Malta for many years (see Chapter 11, Windfalls Abroad) As with the larger square metre class, the fact that several 30 sq m yachts are still sailing today is a measure of how well they were built in the first place some 70 years ago.

SMALL CRAFT

While this book is principally about the Windfall Yachts reference to the many smaller ex German craft is included here to add to the overall picture, particularly as they were included in the Admiralty lists of ex German yachts, given names and were allocated in the same way, later to be found as reparations in remote parts of the globe.

The principal small craft were STAR (STARBOOT) dinghies, of pre war Olympic fame, the 12 square metre SHARPIES (SCHARPIE-JOLLE) and the

10 square metre OLYMPIC (OLYMPIAJOLLE) dinghies. Many hundreds of these craft were built throughout the 1930's for both private owners and the German Government. Of the latter the German Navy had the STAR dinghies, the Luftwaffe the SHARPIES and it was these together with the OLYMPICS that became reparations after the war. In addition to these three classes there were a number of unidentifiable craft described as simply "dinghy" or "10 square metre". Separate from the above a number of SHARPIES were built in 1946 by the boatyard Ratjhes near Kiel from a stock of oak and teak found in the area. These remained at

Star dinghies at Kiel in 1946

the British Kiel Yacht Club until passed on to the British inland sailing clubs in Germany in the mid 1950's.

It is interesting to read of the offshore racing of these yachts in their early days in 1936. In the North Sea Week 50 sq m yachts were considered daring to sail 20 miles offshore to Heligoland and it was wondered if the 100 sq m yachts might sail in the RORC Big Class next year and even if a 150 sq m yacht might enter for the Fastnet Race. Within 13 years there would be both 50 and 100 sq m Windfalls entered in many RORC races including the Fastnet. Indeed it was not long before three of the 100 sq m yachts were to sail the Atlantic and to cap it all the 50 sq m SEEFALKE I sailed to America in 1995, a supreme credit to the yacht's sound design and construction.

SEA SOLDIER SOLO

Ewen Southby-Tailyour recalls "Much to the horror of the General I sailed Sea Soldier single-handed in a race around the Eddystone in the mid 1960s – I thought at the time I was the first to sail a 50 sq m single-handed but I may be wrong. It was certainly viewed with great trepidation by the General (who I did not tell in advance!) although as I came second and didn't break her he allowed me (it wasn't really his decision as I was the sailing master) to do so again".

Two Leading Builders

Abeking and Rasmussen

The yard of Abeking and Rasmussen is generally regarded as a premier builder of Windfalls in quantity and together with Burmester, in quality. Most of the surviving Windfalls today, some seventy years old, were built at this yard. Apart from ROBBE, MERLIN, AVALANCHE and KRANICH all the 100 square metre yachts were built there, as were about thirty-five of the 50 square metre class.

The yard was established by George Abeking and Henry Rasmussen at Lemwerder on the banks of the River Weser in 1907. They developed great expertise in building both power and sailing yachts, in iron or wood up to 160 feet in length. Some, such as the 100 sq m yachts were composite, wood on iron frames. The works was well funded from the beginning, resulting in a well laid out site with a transverse railway and turntable, enabling rapid movement of yachts in and out of the sheds and for launching. Very large stocks of high quality timber were maintained. By the mid 1930s the yards had built well over 3000 sailing and power yachts. They had built up a reputation for good design and high quality workmanship, so it was inevitable that they should be given large orders to build sailing yachts for the Kriegsmarine and Luftwaffe when the requirement arose. Between 1932 and 1939 the yard built 650 craft before transferring fully to war production, then mainly of 120 ft patrol craft.

In the 1970's Abeking and Rasmussen stopped building small craft and concentrated on yachts of 30 metres in length and over. The yard is as busy as ever today, a living reminder that from Edwardian times, through the Windfall era to the modern day, quality will always sell.

Burmester

More correctly, the yard is named Yacht – und Bootswerft Burmester and is situated on the river Weser at Bremen. Although a smaller yard than Abeking and Rasmussen, nevertheless very high quality yachts were built there including some well known and long lasting Windfalls. Amongst these are the 60 ton yawl NORDWIND, the 100 sq m yachts WAL (later MERLIN now ZEEAREND) and ROBBE together with the 26 ton HELGOLAND (PICKLE) and BORKUM (CAPELLA). They also built the 50 sq m Windfalls SEEWOLF (HUSKY), SEEMOWE (TORCH) and SEESCHWALBE (SEA SWALLOW). They also built OSTWIND, a sister ship of NORDWIND but she went to America after the war.

The yard's principal government customer was the Kriegsmarine, for whom they built fourteen yachts in the 1935 to 1939 period of which the eight above subsequently became Windfalls. They built no yachts for the Luftwaffe.

CHAPTER 3. An Eventful 1945

With the ending of hostilities in Europe on 5 May 1945 there naturally was an enormous amount of activity of every sort in all areas of Germany, including supporting the local population, re-establishing basic services, communications etc, complicated by the huge movements of troops and civilians. The City of Kiel was virtually wrecked, there were over 200,000 displaced persons and Prisoners of War in the area to be supported, some of whom were in the 350 ships in Kiel Harbour. The occupying forces were at full stretch – as just one example wrecked factories with gaping roofs were immediately opened and teams set to work making thousands of urgently needed sanitary buckets and also shovels for debris clearance.

One of the tasks of the Royal Navy in Germany was to assemble and dispose of all captured craft which ranged from large naval and merchant ships to dinghies. In practice it was not as simple as that as anyone who has experience of immediate post war situations will know. There is a period of almost lawlessness prior to a return to a more structured regime. Regarding the German yachts in the south Baltic area things were no different. While many yachts had been laid up in centralised areas by the German authorities, others had been kept in isolated areas or even hidden.

It was realised very early on that the great numbers of yachts, particularly the larger ones were valuable and needed to be controlled in some way. The Senior Royal Naval Officer Schleswig Holstein (SNOSH) which included the Kiel and Flensburg areas was Rear Admiral Baille-Grohman, himself a keen sailor and a pre war Chairman of the Royal Naval Sailing Association (RNSA). His staff instigated a survey of all ships, yachts and smaller craft, a large and complicated task particularly where ownership was disputed. Privately owned boats were requisitioned and used by the services in the short term. In due course they were returned to their owners, properly maintained and later a charter fee paid for their

Interrogation party at Kiel May 1945
Commander Jan Aylen 2nd from left

use. Government owned vessels, being legal spoils of war (reparations) were categorised into groups for disposal. There were many difficulties: for example the highly principled German Commanding Officer of the Kriegsmarine School at Murwick, Kapitan Luth, before the war ended, decided to sell the yachts in his domain to German civilians to prevent them falling into the Allies' hands, the money being returned to the German authorities. Unfortunately he was accidentally shot dead by a German sentry shortly after capitulation, leaving a jungle to unravel with the new "owners" of the yachts.

It might seem that a yacht fleet in the south Baltic should have been a low priority in Spring 1945, with war in the Far East still continuing. However with many thousands of British servicemen in Germany who had been through the trauma of years of war and were not yet due to go back to UK, it was very important that they should have an outlet of recreational facilities.

Fortunately, in parallel with this activity a number of senior British officers in the area were themselves keen on sailing and realised the importance of having sailing facilities for the servicemen. Thus the existence of the many sailing clubs and superb yachts proved a godsend and as the dust settled a little, some of the facilities and yachts were quickly put to use. There were a few nautical "irregularities", for example flags of all sorts abounded, the Navy not so gently reminding units that the Union Flag flown in a boat meant that an Admiral of the Fleet was on board.

Colonel W G Fryer RE

Of long standing significance was the almost immediate formation of a yacht club at Kiel, using the facilities of the former Kieler Yacht Club, a prestigious club founded in 1887. As Colonel W G Fryer Royal Engineers put it "I found the Olympia Haven full of yachts and the Kieler Yacht Club locked up and empty. So I told my Chief Engineer and assistant Quarter Master General (AQMG) that I was going to requisition some yachts from the harbour and form a yacht club. They both nodded, so we went ahead." And so in June 1945, only a month after hostilities ceased, the British Kiel Yacht Club was formed, its first Commodore being Captain K L M Robinson RN., Senior Naval Officer Kiel Area. Vice Commodores were Rear Admiral H T Baillie-Grohman and Lt Col E McDonald RE, a most active Sapper yachtsman. Brigadier AG Matthew was an important member, being Commander of the Brigade District. They had a number of very experienced yachtsmen to call on, including Commander "Jan" Aylen and Maj Harvey-Jamieson. The Royal Engineer Yacht Club, always to the fore, made their Baltic Headquarters in the club.

By July 1945 the British Baltic Sailing Association was formed under the chairmanship of Rear Admiral Baillie-Grohman, comprising clubs at Kiel, Eckernforde, Flensburg, Neustadt and on the large Schwerin Lake at Ratzeburg, at Pion and Schlei. And so began the first Windfall season.

British Kiel Yacht Club 1945

Perhaps the first ever race between Windfalls was in June 1945 (or even May), certainly being recorded in the first edition of the Kiel Journal published on 7 July 1945. Six STAR Class boats took part in "pouring rain and very little wind" in a slow race which was won by Major Harvey-Jamieson of 312 Detachment. The next club race from Flensburg to Kiel, a distance of over 50 miles in "6 metre yachts" was also won by him, with Lt Col McDonald, Vice Commodore of the British Kiel Yacht Club, one boat's length behind after 10 hours racing. This passage race to transfer small boats to the more controlled area at Kiel whetted the appetite of those who took part and immediately cruises into the Baltic were planned, using the larger yachts.

There were some very large and fine yachts (above 100 sq m) requisitioned

BKYC card dated 3 June 1945

at that time and were sailed by the occupying services. A few were ex German government owned but several had German owners who were only too happy that their yachts were maintained at such a difficult time. One such was JACUNDA (150 sq m), which became the flagship of the British Kiel Yacht Club. She therefore was a sort of "Honorary Windfall" being sailed by the occupying services but in due course returned to her owner. Other very large yachts were NORDWIND, ALK and SKAGERRAK (all 300 sq m), ASGUARD, ETTSI, JUNGFLIEGER (all 180 sq m), AEGIR X, LIVELY, DORIS, MARGARETHA and SEEBAR (like JACUNDA all 150 sq m) and KAPITEIN HARM (125 sq m). These yachts are described by square metres simply to indicate their relative sizes and are not the actual classifications.

Some of these very large yachts, together with some 100 and 50 sq m craft, were used in the summer of 1945 for early cruises into the Baltic, initially outside Danish waters. When the borders were opened two very successful "cruises in company" were organised by the Royal Navy in conjunction with the Royal Danish Navy, visiting Faarborg, Svendborg and Marstal and led by Commander Aylen in NORDWIND. Army cruises were organised by Major Harvey-Jamieson, using AEGIR X, JACUNDA and others also into Danish waters. North of Kiel the Royal Air Force occupying forces had collected some ex Luftwaffe craft, including some 100 sq m yachts and were using these. To give a flavour of the sheer enjoyment that these craft provided, Commander Aylen wrote the following account of his introduction to NORDWIND in May 1945.

"As summer drew on we moved the little Mess to a delightful office block looking down the long Eckernfurde towards the Baltic. One of the prizes of war was the fleet of some 50 German Naval yachts which were turned over to the Royal Navy, and 30 Assault Unit took on the "NORDWIND", a superb 60 ton Bermudan cutter which had raced well in the 1939 Fastnet Race. She was a splendid yacht for our purpose, as she needed anything from 10 to 20 crew to handle the hefty gear. She drew 13 feet, embarrassing at times in shoal water, and had a spinnaker which seemed like a tennis court in size when broken out. We kept her at a jetty under our noses with two German sailors as ship-keepers. Every week-end we set off into the Baltic exploring the Jutland and Schleswig Holstein coasts, and buying butter and ham in Denmark such as we had not seen for years. It was simply superb sailing. One week-end we took an inexperienced army crew to Svendborg over night, suddenly having to jibe all standing in the dark when an unlit wreck loomed up. At dawn a rather critical lightship on which we had fixed suddenly disappeared completely – it had apparently returned to Svendborg in daylight, a disconcerting custom, as explained by the harbour master. He expressed his horror that we had sailed round the south of Funen and when told about the wreck said "There are 40 wrecks there, and no one knows where they are." NORDWIND had no engine – an advantage in that we had no anxiety about keeping to channels swept of magnetic mines. To skipper a yacht that size was perhaps about the most wonderful climax to a war that anyone could hope for."

60 ton Yawl Nordwind
Beken of Cowes

While these very large yachts looked so fine, there were some practical weak points as Major Harvey-Jamieson wrote in early 1946:

"The pride of the whole fleet was AEGIR X, which had been built for the German Navy. She was an Ocean Racing Bermudian cutter of about 45 tons T.M., LOA 66 feet, draft about 9 ft 6 in, sail area about 1500 square feet. She was a very handsome boat and beautifully built – mahogany planking on steel frames. Her deck layout and deck fittings, however seemed to display an extraordinary lack of practical knowledge. For instance, the runners ended in two parts, the after part had a large hook which fastened to an eyebolt in the deck. The other part led to a purchase along the deck. When running one hand would unhook the after part, take the other out of the sheave, carry the whole lot to the main shrouds where the hook had to be secured. To take in the runner the whole lot had to be reversed: it could be imagined that gybing was no easy matter.

Another extraordinary defect was that there was no possible place for a dinghy except forward of the mast, where it got in the way of the headsail sheets and would have been a menace in any real sea. The obvious place amidships was taken up by a stupid deckhouse which, although large was only a glorified companionway and had not even a seat or a chart table. Later we acquired another boat of the same class, JACUNDA which had belonged to a private owner. Her layout and fittings were much more practical: she had an excellent chart room with two berths, opening out of the cockpit. She was, however, slower than AEGIR, very tender in a squall."

Throughout 1945 the various clubs and organisations became more strongly formed and their individual fleets established. During that year there were inter club sailing matches and many servicemen were introduced to sailing for the first time. The importance of the pre-war Kiel Week was recognised and accordingly a successful first Kiel Week was organised from 31 August to 4 September 1945, which included both class and handicap racing. And so an eventful and highly active summer of sailing drew to a close as the season's end approached.

It was at this point, in September 1945, that there entered on the scene an unusual and highly respected German ex officer – Bruno Splieth, who was to have a profound impact on services sailing at Kiel. He had sailed his minesweeper into Kiel in May and was made a prisoner of war until it was realised that he had skills to offer. An ex coastal freighter skipper at the age of 22, he was a keen sailor and had already won a

Bruno Splieth

National Championship in the Olympic Jolly boat class. He became employed by the British Kiel Yacht Club, firstly as a shipwright and was in time to become "The rock on which the club was built". His love of boats and the sea was infectious and his standards high. Thus at the very time when there were large numbers of very high quality yachts and smaller craft to be sorted out at Kiel he arrived at an ideal time.

(To run ahead briefly Bruno, a Master Mariner, was employed as a shipwright, Yacht Master, Harbour Master and Sailing Master over the next 38 years. He continued his competitive sailing, becoming Starboat German Champion eight times and winner of the folkboat World Championship Gold Cup. He competed in three Olympics and was National Coach in 1972 and 1976, later becoming a member of the Olympic Sailing committee. A natural communicator, he was a perfect choice to provide continuity at the yacht club where so much adventure training was carried out with thousands of young people over the years. He loved sailing the Windfall yachts from Kiel and took a particular pride in their upkeep. For years he would always extend a special welcome when others came in from UK. In 1970 he was awarded the MBE, a very popular selection and when he retired in 1982 was made an honorary member of the Royal Engineer Yacht Club, The Royal Artillery Yacht Club and the Royal Signals Yacht Club. He was the first Honorary Rear Commodore for life of the British Kiel Yacht Club. Bruno died in 1990 and the Spieth Regatta is held in his memory to this day. He was a central figure in the Windfall story at Kiel).

To return to 1945, throughout that year representations were made to Headquarters Germany and to London that some of the yacht fleet should be despatched to England for use by the services there. There was a need to reduce the numbers in the Baltic generally to preserve the yachts and to ease the maintenance load while at the same time taking advantage of a once only opportunity to equip the services in UK with modern yachts for training. And so it came about that in parallel with the highly successful activity on the water in the Baltic there arose a number of administrative issues which eventually reached a very high level indeed both in Germany at the Supreme Allied Headquarters Expeditionary Force and in the Admiralty, Air Ministry and Treasury in England. Briefs were given to the First Sea Lord and the Chief of the Air Staff in Germany.

The main issue was who "owned" the ex German government yachts. One of Rear Admiral Baillie-Grohman's tasks, as Senior Naval Officer Schleswig Holstein (SNOSH) was the assembly, control and distribution of all shipping in his area. In the case of sailing craft the practical way to do this was where possible to encourage units to form sailing clubs, often in previous club premises, and look after the boats in their area themselves. This was put on a formal footing in June 1945 by Flag Officer Western Germany, with all ex German Government owned yachts being classified as warships pending decisions on their final disposal. It so happened that some ex Luftwaffe yachts, which included an 85 ft steel schooner DUHNEN (1912) and four of the fine 100 square metre class, were sailed and looked after by the Royal Air Force Occupying Forces. See Appendix 5. As the

ex Luftwaffe 50 sq m Sperling
Beken of Cowes

year went on the RAF, through their administrative authorities in Germany and to the Air Ministry in UK, made their point that all captured ex Luftwaffe property would become the property of the RAF. In particular the yachts that they were using in Germany should be transferred to the RAF in UK in due course.

The Royal Navy in Germany took a different view; anything that floated was the responsibility of the Royal Navy and they should be the one authority for the administration of all the yachts and smaller craft, particularly with the increasing requirement to sail many of the yachts to UK for use there. While it was fully agreed that in the Baltic all three services should use the craft in their areas, the matter of sailing yachts to UK waters was a naval affair to administer. There were very many issues to be sorted – the safe passage arrangements, refitting and equipping the yachts, qualification and formation of crews, etc etc.

Matters rather came to a head in October 1945 when literally out of the blue over fifty RAF Officers were flown by Coastal Command Sunderland flying boats from RAF Calshot in the Solent to Schlei, intending to sail nine ex Luftwaffe yachts home. The first that Rear Admiral Baillie-Grohman knew of it was when the Resident Naval Officer at Schlei rang him to say that nine yachts were due to sail at 0600 next day. The Admiral immediately rang his RAF counterpart, Air Vice Marshall Trail of 83 Group and informed him that he would have appreciated notice of this operation, "that in his opinion it was too late in the season to sail from east to west, especially with the swept channels as they were and in any case they would need more than racing sails". The Air Vice Marshall said that he could not agree, that "surely the Admiral was exaggerating and the yachts were being handled by very experienced yachtsmen. Also the Air Ministry had approval from the Admiralty".

The sequel did no credit to anyone but is recorded here as part of the Windfall history. The nine yachts duly sailed with RAF crews, went through the Kiel Canal to Cuxhaven and from there set off for UK, against the advice of the local Admiral. Within 36 hours eight of the yachts were back in Cuxhaven, some with damaged equipment and from there the crews were immediately flown home in three Sunderland aircraft. Bad weather and seasickness had taken their toll, which could have happened to any crews no matter which service they came from. The eight yachts were left in the care of the Royal Navy for the winter. The ninth yacht, an 85 ft steel schooner DUHNEN reached UK but was found not to be an ex Luftwaffe yacht and was reported as being impounded by Admiralty marshals. So ended this spirited "Dawn Raid" which would have been best avoided.

Looking back, if ever there was a case for the formation of one Ministry of Defence this was one example. At both high level and ground level there was no problem but somehow between the Admiralty and Air Ministry and thence down the chain of command messages were interpreted differently. In practice of course the ex German yachts were not "owned" by any individual service but by the UK Government, with the Treasury having a final say. Equally, as Rear Admiral Baillie-Grohman reported, if the RN and the RAF claimed "Their" yachts there would have been none for the Army, which was plainly nonsense. As we shall see in Chapter 6, all three services in UK were in due course allocated their fair share of craft through a tri-service organisation according to their needs.

And so an eventful 1945 drew to a close. Despite the pleas by the Royal Naval staff in Germany to allow the magnificent yachts NORDWIND, SKAGERRAK and others to be sailed to UK, the only Windfall to do so in that year was the DUHNEN. Above all else the yachts and smaller craft had provided the occupying forces with tremendously enjoyable recreational sailing in Germany, greatly helping morale at a difficult time when servicemen were naturally looking towards home. Numerous sailing clubs had been established from which to race and explore Baltic waters, while many craft had been brought to sailing condition after six years of lay up. Preparations were in hand towards what was to be an equally busy 1946 when most of the yachts were to be sailed or transported to UK and the Windfall era in home waters set to begin.

CHAPTER 4. 1946 – Operations Homeward and Sallyport

To go back briefly in time, on 21 May 1945, less than three weeks after hostilities in Europe ceased, Rear Admiral Baillie-Grohman, as Senior Naval Officer Schleswig Holstein, had written to the Allied Naval commander in Germany suggesting that the valuable ex German Navy 300 square metre yachts OSTWIND, NORDWIND and SKAGGERAK be sailed at the first opportunity to UK, together with some smaller ones which may be found, to prevent them being looted or knocked about. This was not agreed in the short term by the Admiralty, who had many other issues to deal with, not the least a continuing war in the Far East. Further letters followed to the Admiralty during 1945 asking for a decision on the government owned yachts and disposal instructions, sowing the seeds in UK that it would make sense to bring home many of the German yachts for use by units from all three services. As we have seen this was translated in some quarters to a go ahead for some of the ex Luftwaffe yachts to sail in late 1945.

It was in January 1946 that Rear Admiral Baillie-Grohman wrote to the British Naval Commander in Chief Germany and to the Admiralty with specific proposals for the transfer of the ex German government yachts to the UK and their subsequent allocation. This far reaching paper titled OPERATION HOMEWARD proposed that, having discussed this with UK authorities, the Commander in Chief Portsmouth should be put in charge of the reception of the yachts at Portsmouth and for their care and maintenance until they were allocated or sold. That the destination of all yachts should be Portsmouth. That Captain G C Phillips, GM, DSO RN, currently Commanding Officer of HMS Dolphin in Portsmouth and also Chairman of the Royal Naval Sailing Association (RNSA) should act as "Rear Link" and with his working committee be the authority for selecting yacht skippers and organising delivery crews. That recommendations for the allocation of the yachts be provided by the newly formed joint service Association of Service Yacht Clubs under the Chairmanship of Admiral Sir Geoffrey Blake, KCB, DSO, co-opting civilian clubs if necessary. That in the case of naval personnel the time they spent absent in collecting the yachts should not be counted as part of their annual leave. Finally the question of the ex Luftwaffe yachts should be given urgent attention.

There followed in February the initial full list of ex Kriegsmarine yachts recommended for transfer to the UK, together with their ten or so current locations in the Schleswig Holstein area. It was divided into two lists, A and B, A being the very largest yachts for movement in early May. That the situation was fluid is demonstrated that one of the A List yachts, OSTWIND, sister ship to NORDWIND in fact ended up with the American forces and was transferred to the USA. The list of yachts was to be continually modified and by April a combined list was issued by the Vice Admiral Commanding British Naval forces Germany, naming both ex Kriegsmarine and ex Luftwaffe craft. The majority of the yachts (about sixty), mainly ex Kriegsmarine, would be sailed under the Royal Naval OPERATION HOMEWARD to Portsmouth. In addition over a hundred smaller craft, from 30 sq m down to dinghies would be shipped during the year to UK in PLUTO, which was probably a name for a Tank Landing Craft but the records only give them numbers. Those ex Luftwaffe yachts (about fourteen) previously sailed in the Baltic from sailing clubs of the occupying RAF forces would be sailed to UK under the Royal Air Force OPERATION SALLYPORT to Calshot in the Solent.

Meanwhile the Royal Air Force was making independent plans to sail the eight ex Luftwaffe yachts from Cuxhaven and six from Schleswig in March 1946. However following a meeting between the Admiral and Air Vice Marshall Trail in February it was agreed that this proposal would be cancelled and the yachts would be included in the general plan for sailing. In this way the sailing orders, routeing, provision of equipment, escort arrangements if applicable, crew qualification etc would be controlled under one naval umbrella. The Navy would also provide assistance in ensuring that these craft were seaworthy and supplying a small amount of canvas and stores.

HMS Savage

OPERATION HOMEWARD, was carried out throughout the 1946 season in a series of nine groups of yachts, the naval crews being shipped out by a number of destroyers, the first being HMS SAVAGE in early May. The call for naval volunteers to sail this batch of eleven yachts home was promulgated under Portsmouth General Order (PGO) 7982 (These orders are shown at Appendix 9) together with the arrangements for the first batch under PGO 8041.

It may be imagined that after the tremendous pressures of war the operations must have had a great appeal to sailors – being paid for a yacht passage cruise. Of course it was not as simple as that and the crews had many adventures between them. While most of the yachts' hulls were in good condition, there were certainly defects in the sails and running rigging. Most yachts had no engine and of course going westwards in the North Sea and Channel in wooden yachts of generally low freeboard meant many a wet trip. That year there were some particularly heavy storms in August.

POKER DICE

Patrick Fryer was one of 40 volunteers who embarked aboard HMS COMUS in July 1946 to collect and sail back just eleven of the yachts – two 100 sq ms and nine 50 sq m. He subsequently recalled: "The voyage to Kiel was not without its amusing side. The volunteers fell into three categories – experienced yachtsmen, those with some sailing experience, mostly dinghy sailing in sheltered waters, and complete novices . . . the experienced yachtsmen were keen to enlist those with similar experience while the dinghy sailors and novices were equally anxious to crew a skipper with experience – which necessitated concealing their own inexperience. This led to an interesting game of conversational poker dice."

Records of early 1946 are sketchy but on 15 April it was reported from Kiel that "12 Star Class dinghies were to be shipped in PLUTO when she returns". It is not clear therefore whether she had already made a delivery trip but from then on she was continuously ferrying small craft up to 30 sq m size to UK.

And so the great yacht exodus got under way. First to sail in May were the fine yachts SKAGERRAK (Lieutenant Commander Taylor, King's Harbourmaster at Kiel) and NORDWIND (Commander Aylen) with a crew of seventeen. At the same time it was signalled to UK from Naval Headquarters in Berlin that ADLER (later GALAHAD) and four 50 sq m were ready with probably three more. The first batch of 50 sq m yachts sailed on 15 May, including SEE TAUBE (later DISDAINE) with the convivial Lt Morin Scott, RNR as skipper. In addition the large yachts ASTA, HELGOLAND and ORION were on stand by. A second destroyer, HMS ORWELL, brought out more naval crews on 29 May, arriving at Kiel on 3 June. It was apparent that briefing for the trip could have been clearer as some brought their own food and were pleasantly surprised

50 sq m Disdaine (ex Seetaube)
Beken of Cowes

(they should surely have known) that Naval small ships are wonderfully adept in producing good food in all weathers.

100 sq m Sea Lion (ex Luftwaffe yacht Austernfischer)
Beken of Cowes

The Royal Air Force were quickly into action and were also to sail in June under the code name OPERATION SALLYPORT. It was on 29 May that crews for 14 yachts including four of the 100 square metre class were flown to Schleswig and Cuxhaven by Sunderland flying boats and they sailed in mid June. Not all went smoothly and the 100 sq m AUSTERNFISCHER (Squadron Leader E R G Gouldie), sailing from Cuxhaven, got into trouble in a gale off Dungeness, twice having to repair her torn sails. When it happened a third time they called for assistance from a cargo boat, getting a tow first from HMS BAMBOROUGH CASTLE then a fishing boat, arriving in Folkstone on 17 June. Interestingly the ex German skipper of the yacht, Kurt Koppler, was in the crew, together with Wing Commander H P Russell-Smith and Flight Lieutenant D E Breed, all being mentioned in an article in The Times. Some other yachts in the group turned back to Cuxhaven but eventually after various experiences they all reached Calshot, the last (the 50 sq m PIROL) arriving on 29 June. A perceptive shortened account of her voyage from Schleswig by two airmen in her crew may be seen at Appendix 11. It must be remembered that there were large numbers of high speed craft in RAF Coastal Command for air sea rescue so knowledge of conditions at sea was not entirely the prerogative of the Senior Service. Indeed during that same week, KORSAR (Skipper Major Norman Tailyour, later Commandant General Royal Marines), having almost reached Ijmuiden had to turn tail and run all the way back to Borkum under storm jib. Force 11 was recorded that night.

While a number of the yachts were in good condition, having been sailed regularly in 1945, there were many still laid up and without masts and equipment. Thus throughout the winter of 1945 and throughout 1946 there was a considerable task to prepare the yachts for sailing or transit to UK. By Spring 1946 it became apparent that there was a need to have a dedicated team to formally speed up this work. And so it was in May 1946 that Martyn Sherwood, promoted to Acting Commander for the job, arrived on the scene at Kiel from UK, having been appointed with the express task of organising the yachts for dispatch and refitting those that still needed it. Sherwood was a natural choice for the job – a piratical character with a strong personality who was one of a group of

Commander Martyn Sherwood

Peter Richardson

naval officers who had the yacht TAI MO SHAN built in Hong Kong and sailed her home in the 1920's. As Senior Naval Officer (Yachts) at Kiel he set to with a will and quickly became a central figure in the Windfall story of that time.

Joining with Sherwood was newly promoted Lieutenant Peter Richardson RN, a keen and lively officer who had been awarded the DSC the year before at the age of twenty. He was an experienced sailor for his age and was to make four (possibly five) delivery trips to UK in different yachts, two of them as skipper. As a result of these experiences he was to regularly sail Windfalls in UK, particularly SEA OTTER of which he was very fond. In due course, after most successful usage by the Navy she was sold in 1958 and it was Peter who bought her, changing her name back to the original SEEOTTER, keeping her until he died in 2002.

Sherwood quickly realised that there was a need for the very varied crews to have a shake down cruise locally in the Baltic first to get familiar with their craft before sailing to UK. Basing himself in MARABU, a particularly high quality 100 sq m yacht (incidentally built for the Luftwaffe but that seemed to have escaped notice by the higher authorities), he led from the front and is remembered to this day by those who took part in the operation. Using British and German personnel he and his team rapidly expanded the refitting capacity, no mean achievement considering the wide variety of yachts to be made seaworthy and shortage of sails and spares.

From mid 1946 many stories were rife, embellished as the years went on, about large numbers of yachts being

50 sq m Meon Maid (ex Drossel)
Beken of Cowes

found hidden all over the area at that time. It is true that in the early days in 1945 not only were civilians hiding yachts but also occupying forces units hiding them from each other! However it was now a year since the first Windfalls were gathered and while a number were found secreted in 1946 very few new Windfalls were found from this time. One exception was when Peter Richardson found a 30 square metre Windfall hidden in a barn and covered with hay. It was recovered and in due course was used by the services in Malta. Then at Travenmunde he and a friend found a yacht aground and apparently abandoned on the Russian side of the estuary. They swam across, surveyed it and later that night returned with a rope and a 10 ton truck. "Rescuing" the yacht, the 39 sq m JOASS, Peter was apparently left to sail the boat to Kiel himself while the truck was returned. From Travenmunde to Kiel is about 70 miles, in which case this must have been quite a trip in itself but so many adventures were taking place at that time that it may not

have been that unusual. He later recalled that in the Autumn Martyn Sherwood decided he wanted to sail the yacht to England himself and apparently set off wearing a chef's hat, stripped to the waist and beating his midriff with a wooden spoon. Peter was glad that with Martyn gone the show at Kiel was now his but this was dispelled by a dispatch rider who came from Cuxhaven with a message from Martyn. Fortunately it turned out to be simply a note for Peter to send a genoa left on the quay. The whole is an unlikely story but whatever the true sequel, JOASS did indeed arrive in England via Chatham and was to give good service in the Mediterranean. She was one of the smaller yachts to be sailed to UK.

50 sq m Leopard (ex Norbec)
Beken of Cowes

Two more batches of yachts with naval crews sailed in June and by July OPERATION HOMEWARD was running smoothly, as can be seen by the more organised structure of the paperwork on file. The 50 sq m yachts DROSSELL (Cdr Brooks), MOSQUITO (Lt Brooks), GUNTHER (Cdr Pringle) sailed on 2 July, followed later in the month by the 100 sq m ROBBE (Cdr Fryer) and the 50 sq m yachts BRUNHILDE (Lt Mair RNVR), SEEJUNGFER (Lt Wilson), ZEISIG (Lt Scott RNR), SEEFALKE II (Lt McColgan) and HILTGUND (Cdr Saunders RNVR), who sailed independently and arrived at Ramsgate due to stress of weather.

Crews for the 5th phase of OPERATION HOMEWARD sailed in the destroyer CYGNET in early August. It was during this month that the worst weather of the season developed and NORBEC (Lt Crossley) was to be caught out badly in a storm, the yacht abandoned but salvaged by her Dutch rescuers. A vivid account of this episode by Lt Cdr Fryer is attached at Appendix 13.

Wotan (later Martlet) in the Dutch canals 1946

Few yachts were reported having sailed at that time although SEEBRISE (Capt D Stroud RM) did leave Wilhelmshaven on the 30th August followed by NECK (Lt Hazell RNVR) from there a week later. Like JOASS, NECK (later NIMROD) a centre board 39 sq m yacht was one of the smaller craft sailed back.

A curious anomaly arose here. With SEEBRISE at Wilhelmshaven was WOTAN (later MARTLET), skippered by Cdr Jago. They duly sailed, WOTAN was dismasted and although unusually the yacht had an engine it was unserviceable and they were towed into Den Helder. Jago signalled that they were going to Amsterdam to refit, the crew returning to UK. She went to Rotterdam and on 15 September Jago sent in his damage report. At this stage Cdr Sherwood at Kiel opted to bring WOTAN to UK when she was repaired but it is unlikely that he did so. In any event the next report stated that WOTAN arrived in Portsmouth on 14 November. All these events are documented by current signals.

Meanwhile back in August crews from the Royal Naval College Dartmouth, led by Lieut Peyton-Jones, had travelled to Portsmouth and collected the six 50 sq m yachts allocated to the College and sailed them there during the summer leave. Included was the 50 sq m yacht under her new name MARTLET. Now MARTLET was ex WOTAN so the mystery is still with us. It could not have been WOTAN that the cadets sailed west: perhaps her allocation to the college was temporally filled by the 50 sq m MOSQUITO, who certainly sailed with the little fleet but was never heard of again. By 1947 WOTAN, now MARTLET was firmly in the college 50 sq m Windfall fleet and remained so until they were replaced in 1959.

Martyn Sherwood helming Marabu

COMMON CURRENCY

Time and time again in correspondence from those who collected Windfalls there was reference to the currency in use at the time. Tobacco. Morin Scott, who sailed both SEETAUBE and ZEISIG home from Kiel, wrote "In Cuxhaven, a great deal of entertainment resulted and the ridiculousness of the situation was demonstrated when, one evening, I entertained all the crews of the four yachts to dinner at the local club. The twenty of us enjoyed a good meal with wine and then, on calling for the bill, found that I had left my wallet on board. No problem, I merely called for cigars and when these had been offered round I took half a dozen outside the club and sold them to the first available buyer before returning with enough money to pay the bill and last me the rest of the evening".

Eventually nine batches of yachts were sailed in 1946 under OPERATION HOMEWARD, the last one in September (although stragglers WOTAN and LADY EVE arrived later). Included in that batch was CAPELLA (Capt John Wells) and MARABU, skippered by Martyn Sherwood with Peter Richardson as Mate. Between them they had achieved a great deal, adding both organisational skills and colour to the Windfall story at a turbulent time, all in only four months.

No apology is offered for including here and in the Appendices a few direct abbreviated accounts of a number of very different passages to UK, which ranged from 3 days to 2 months. They are included, with grateful thanks to the authors, to give a flavour by those actually there at the time. The first is a very brief and modest account by the then Lt Cdr H N Taylor, King's Harbour Master at Kiel in 1946.

SKAGERRAK

"I think it was in May 1946 that I took the SKAGERRAK, with her volunteer crew, into Holtenau lock for passage to England. We had one or two other prizes towing through the canal, one of which developed defects and had to be left behind in Rendsberg. We left the canal and went on to Cuxhaven to spend the night tied up alongside, and I was able to visit my brother in the wardroom of the naval party there. Next day we set out on our own to Portsmouth – quite an ordinary sail, which took us about two and a half days. Arriving at Portsmouth, I was ordered to hand SKAGGERAK over to the Captain of HMS REVENGE, moored off Priddy's Hard . . . I was soon at home in Brockenhurst with my various offerings from Denmark which included an eleven pound Danish blue cheese".

Similarly Commander Jan Aylen wrote:

NORDWIND

I had a final trip to Kiel to arrange the return passage of NORDWIND to UK. She had been completely re-rigged and given new sails under reparations payment. I had a crew of seventeen with my old sailing master, Patrick Phibbs as mate. We were towed through the Kiel Canal, and from Cuxhaven to Portsmouth was an uneventful three day passage, including one becalmed.

One very rewarding aspect of researching Windfalls has been the renewal of old friendships through the correspondence involved. This is part of a letter from Pat Fryer to Morin Scott 45 years after they brought back two Windfalls through the Dutch canals and reflects the mood of the time.

ZEISIG (SEA SCAMP) and NORBEC (LEOPARD) in HAALEM

50 sq m Sea Scamp (ex Zeisig)
Beken of Cowes

I mainly remember the trip, at times, as a hilarious adventure to which you were the main contributor. Do you remember the night we spent in Haalem? There was no wind and the rain was teeming down and we were all soaked to the skin. We made fast to a lamppost – had hot toddies all round – several in fact and went ashore with both crews. You with a bottle of brandy and me with one of whisky. Ashore we found the town in festive mood celebrating its 700th Anniversary with an enormous fair.

Our entry into the fair began with you trying to strike the bell at the top of one of those towers and when you failed to do so you began to strip down to the waist, raining blow after blow. This quickly collected a large crowd and the attendant let you go on reckoning that it would pay him to let you do so. Finally you did, I think, succeed and then visited several side shows but somehow became separated from our crews. But we both retained our whisky and brandy and were followed by the crowd which had watched you with the mallet. We finished up at after midnight on the Dodgem cars by which time we had disposed of much of the contents of the bottles. You eventually tried to climb the pole of the dodgem which connected with the network of electric wires above. At that point we were ordered off and, I think, escorted out of the fairground.

We then found ourselves on the road back to the canal. I remember sitting with you on the kerb where there were some road works guarded by a hurricane lamp which we used to read the name of the road – you were convinced that we were in Piccadilly! We eventually arrived back at our yachts which were moored side by side and you insisted on seeing me down the fore hatch and safely into my bunk. Then I insisted on doing the same for you. I don't know how many times we saw each other into our bunks but when I looked down your hatch next morning you were lying on your bunk, fully clothed and wringing wet – you had ended by falling into the canal. I don't know how you managed to get out.

NEWHAVEN SUPPLIES

SEETAUBE was sailed home by Morin Scott and a sociable crew, their last night in Kiel spent at a party in the yacht club, at one point swinging on the glass chandeliers. Eventually, weeks later they put into Newhaven. "Our penultimate stop was Newhaven, from where I nipped home to get a car and then drove to Eastbourne where there was a Naval Establishment entirely manned by the Paymaster branch. Announcing myself as 'the Commanding Officer of SEETAUBE, prize of war on passage under sail from Kiel to Portsmouth, delayed by westerly winds' I demanded rations for a mythical crew of much enlarged proportion for the long passage against the wind to Portsmouth. On being asked to estimate the time required, I estimated two weeks, possibly three as the weather was bad.

The whiff of romantic salt air in the staid "Pusser" organisation worked wonders and in no time mountains of food were loaded into my car and with a few flourishing signatures I was off back to Newhaven. It took nearly two days to parcel up all the food and post it off to various closely rationed families before sailing overnight to Portsmouth and handing over our Prize of War to the receiving officer at Whale Island".

And so the very busy year of 1946 drew to a close. The objective to bring the Windfalls home had been achieved, with no loss of life or yacht which was a great credit to the seamanship of the crews, the quality of the yachts and the overall organisation. There were various rumours of yachts being lost on the Goodwins but like so many tales they were unfounded. With their low freeboards the yachts had proved to be wet but of sound design and tremendous fun to sail. Already by August the yachts were to be seen sailing and racing at Dartmouth, Plymouth and in the Solent. The metamorphosis was complete: what had been a German fleet was now British, with new names for most of the yachts. Such are the side effects of war, but at least achieved peacefully with great good will between sailors of the two countries which has remained to this day. And so the seeds were sown: the word went round the services that here was a fleet of yachts which everyone with a will to sail in them could do so.

Leaving the British Kiel Yacht Club Marina 1946

CHAPTER 5. Windfall Allocation

By mid 1946 the disagreements about the principles of the distribution of the yachts between the services, whether they were ex Kriegsmarine or ex Luftwaffe, had been resolved. Very sensibly the Admiralty, War Office and Air Ministry agreed with the recommendations from Germany that the organisation to propose the yacht allocation should be the newly formed Association of Service Yacht Clubs (ASYC). This was (and still is) a joint service organisation whose function was to co-ordinate service yacht club and sailing association activities. The Chairman was Admiral Sir Geoffrey Blake and the Secretary Group Captain Haylock, later to become Commodore of the RAF Yacht Club and Editor of Yachting Monthly. Both much respected, they had close contact with the Royal Naval Sailing Association (RNSA) who were albeit unofficial advisers to the Admiralty on sailing matters.

It is evident from letters between the two associations that the yacht allocation to all three services was done very fairly taking into account their needs. To quote part of one from Captain Phillips RN, Chairman of the RNSA to Group Captain Haylock dated 19 June 1946: "*I am under the impression that the* (individual) *Service Yacht Clubs think that the RNSA is going to be responsible or partly so, for the allocation of the German yachts coming over to this country. As this is not so, I would be grateful if you could inform them in the sense of the remarks which follow ... It is the wish of the RNSA that all services shall benefit from the acquisition of these yachts and I have said so to anyone who might help in that direction, notably the Admiralty Committee who are in entire agreement.*"

Very Large Yachts

The very large yachts which had been sailed to UK, with their high potential maintenance costs and deep drafts were not considered by the Admiralty to be suitable for service sailing (to the chagrin of a number of sailors, particularly those who crewed these beautiful yachts across). Accordingly and two 300 sq m yachts NORDWIND and SKAGERRAK together with the 85 foot steel schooner DUHNEN were sold soon after their arrival in UK. A most controversial accident occurred to the beautiful SKAGERRAK when she sank at her moorings in Portsmouth Harbour two weeks after her arrival from Germany. Naturally there was a detailed enquiry but the likely cause was the yacht gradually back filling through a head's sea cock combined with a lack of a designated ship keeper to regularly check the boat. It was an expensive lesson re-learned and a great pity after having survived six years of war.

The only very large Windfall to be used by the services in UK was ORION, a Bermudan Cutter of some 60 tons, built in 1910 and she was allocated to the

Edith VII

Royal Navy in the Clyde for a period. She took part in the first post war (1947) Fastnet race crewed by members of the RNSA then had a major refit but soon became uneconomic and was sold.

ASTA, EDITH VII, GODECKE MICHAEL and PAUL BENECKE were sailed back by naval crews but after that not sailed by the services in UK and remained unallocated by the Admiralty in 1947.

At Kiel three very large 150 sq m yachts remained for a while used by the services, and in 1948 AEGIR X, LIVELY and JACUNDA (the British Kiel Yacht Club's flagship) were still there. It was not long however before they were disposed of, no doubt due to the problems of running costs, and thereafter offshore sailing from Kiel was carried out mainly in the more manageable 100 sq m and 50 sq m yachts. It should be remembered that virtually all the yachts, including the 300 sq m craft, had no engine. The very large yachts are included in the list at Appendix 4.

Miscellaneous Yachts

A number of these yachts were sailed over to UK in Operations HOMEWARD and SALLYPORT and are included in Appendix 4. A number were old, being built in the 1920s and some even earlier. The 50 ft ketch KORMORAN was sailed by the Royal Air Force for a number of years including to the Mediterranean. A favourite Windfall at Kiel was the 42 ft ketch RASMUS, a comfortable cruising yacht that was to remain in service hands there for the next 40 years. SIGRID, a 20 ton ketch dating from about 1912, went to the Clyde where she continued for ten years. Two extremely successful Windfalls of this group over many years were CAPELLA (ex BORKUM) and GALAHAD (ex ADLER), both of about 90 sq m. The former had a long

Galahad deck scene.
Mike Jones on helm

career in with the RNVR and in the Solent before going to the Britannia Royal Naval College Dartmouth where she was to continue after the college 50 sq m yachts were replaced in 1959. GALAHAD was to be the principal Windfall at the Royal Naval Engineering College from 1947 to 1960 when she was replaced by a new Sail Training Craft.

100 sq m Yachts

There were ten of these fine yachts to be allocated and were to form the backbone of the service entries in Class 1 racing. Two, MARABU and WAL (later briefly COLLINGWOOD then back to WAL before assuming later her more well known name MERLIN in 1960) were retained by the RN. There was a hiccup with WAL, built for the Kriegsmarine but apparently sold to a private owner but this problem was ironed out by giving him KONIGIN instead and WAL was to give many years service as a Windfall. PELIKAN and STORCH were allocated to the Royal Engineer Yacht Club who renamed them OVERLORD and AVALANCHE respectively. REIHER (GLADEYE later EISVOGEL) went to the Household Division and ROBBE initially to the School of Infantry before going to the Royal Military College Sandhurst. KRANICH (KRANICH) and FLAMINGO remained at the British Kiel Yacht Club for use by the occupying services in the Baltic. Finally AUSTERNFISCHER, now SEA LION, went to RAF Transport Command. These yachts, together with the more numerous 50 square metre class, were to be the true offshore Windfall Fleet for years to come.

Merlin (ex Wal) in the 1960's with a coach roof

50 sq m Yachts

Nearly forty of these yachts became Windfalls, most sailed to UK. They, with the 100 sq m yachts, formed the core of Windfall sailing in the UK services and gave most servicemen their first experience of offshore sailing. The relatively large number of 50 sq m yachts provided the advantages of giving class racing and common spares support. In UK about twenty were allocated to the Royal

Navy, mainly at the Naval Colleges, establishments in the Solent area and outlying units around the country. SEEMOWE,(TORCH),BRUNHILDE (BRYNMERE), SEEFALKE II (SEA EAGLE later SEA FALCON), THEODORA (THEODORIC) and SEEMELKE (ROSANNA) went to the Army while LERCHE, GOLDAMER and MEISE were retained by the Royal Air Force Yacht Club with SPERLING going to RAF Training Command and PIROL to RAF Coastal Command. Two more of the yachts were to go to Canada and one to New Zealand, the remainder staying at Kiel or in one or two cases were lost track of.

The following six yachts were collected from Portsmouth by crews from the Royal Naval College Dartmouth during Summer leave in 1946.

50 sq m Windfall Pegasus (ex Hiltgund)
Beken of Cowes

German Name	English Name	College House
SEEJUNGFER	GRIFFIN*	Grenville
SEESTURM	HAWK	Hawke
WOTAN	MARTLET	Drake
HILTGUND	PEGASUS	St Vincent
NORBEC	LEOPARD	Exmouth
GUNTHER	HARPY**	Benbow

*GRIFFIN was a strange choice of name because the Royal Ocean Racing Club's yacht had long been GRIFFIN, which led to some confusion in the RORC offshore Races, for which the college yacht was described as GRIFFIN (V26), referring to her sail number. Sensibly in 1949 her name was changed to GRYPHIS. When the Dartmouth yachts were replaced with new yachts (named Sail Training Craft) in 1959 she was transferred to the Naval Air Branch and again renamed, this time as KESTREL.

**The yachts were all 50 sq m class except for HARPY, which although originally listed as a 50 sq m class in her 1946 allocation, was in fact slightly different from the others and came to be rated separately. She was the only one of the college yachts of this size to have an engine. One unsolved mystery has been the reference to a 50 sq m named MOSQUITO, mentioned in an OPERATION HOMEWARD report as having been sailed from Germany in early 1946. She was mentioned again in the Christmas 1946 Naval College magazine as having sailed to Dartmouth with the yachts above, having arrived at Dartmouth "full of water because the cadets could not find the pump". Thereafter there has been no reference to MOSQUITO and she has never appeared in any Admiralty references to date. From the start the Naval College yachts at Dartmouth and Plymouth were deemed to be for formal Sail Training and therefore their support was fully funded by the Admiralty, a great advantage when it came to maintenance and sail replacement.

30 sq m Yachts

This class was particularly suited to the waters of the Baltic and many were kept there from 1945 onwards, initially based at the various Baltic yacht clubs. In 1951 most were centralised at the British Kiel Yacht Club, now located at Stickenhorn and these are shown in the master list at Appendix 3. They were also very suited for sailing at Malta and over a period eleven 30 sq m yachts were based there, starting in 1946 with GOTE and SEEJUNGFER. Split between the various services sailing clubs on the island they enjoyed very good class racing there over a number of years.

A few 30 sq m Windfalls were retained in UK. Some, including OSTERLING, ERIDA, SACHSE and MURWIC II were sailed in the Solent area, while LADY ELSA was allocated to Rosyth.

30 sq m Gernet in Malta

SMALL CRAFT

At the end of the war all small craft, both privately and German owned, were requisitioned for recreational use by the occupying forces. In 1946 the Admiralty decreed that in addition to the larger yachts, all ex German government owned small craft were to be transferred to UK where it was felt that there might be a national need for them from civilian as well as service sailing clubs. This produced an understandable reaction from the three services in Germany, whose many sailing clubs relied on these small craft for recreation. The Army in particular, as prime users, made a strong case for the retention of some craft and in due course this was agreed. A number of STAR class dinghies were left in the Baltic for service clubs to use "Until the end of the Occupation". The diverse distribution of just a few of these small craft can be seen in the following documented allocation by Admiralty Fleet Order in December 1947:

HONG KONG	8 STARS
SINGAPORE	4 STARS
BERMUDA (RN)	1 STAR
	1 OLYMPIC
ARMY	13 OLYMPICS
	6 SHARPIES
RAF	14 OLYMPICS
	8 Dinghies
	ex Luftwaffe dinghies, mainly SHARPIEs
RN	10 X 10 Square Metre
	6 OLYMPICS
	2 STARS

In addition there were a very large number of small craft not swept up in this allocation and servicemen remember these craft in other areas, from the South African Station, throughout the Far East, the Mediterranean, the Baltic to many UK sailing clubs such as in the Solent. These small craft were to be found in a variety of unexpected places such as some OLYMPIC dinghies on the Thames for the use of RMA Sandhurst and more at Loch Rescobie in Angus where there was a naval apprentices' sailing club. They are fondly remembered as powerful boats with a good carrying capacity but having a single large mainsail carried considerable weather helm in a blow. These were sailing at Rescobie until 1970 when they were disposed of locally.

Ex German Olympic dinghies on Loch Rescobie, Angus in the 1960s

CHAPTER 6. 1947–1950. The Post War Period

Conditions in the 1940s

It is worth recalling at this stage that offshore sailing 60 years ago was somewhat different from that of today yet in a way more adventurous because there were far fewer aids. Greater time was spent on hull and equipment maintenance, there being no fibreglass yachts: it was twenty years before round the world yachtsmen Francis Chichester, Alec Rose and Robin Knox-Johnson raised the general public's interest in offshore sailing. Until 1945 when the first Sydney to Hobart Race took place, there were just two regular long distance offshore races – the Bermuda Race and the Fastnet, in alternate years. Windfalls were to take part in both.

There were virtually no public marinas: few yachts had engines so it was normal practice to enter small harbours or anchor under sail. There was no system of qualifications for skippers, mates or crew. Perhaps the most significant difference was the requirement for a full time navigator. Sailing offshore required constant plotting of estimated positions based on distance run from a rotating log trailed astern, taking into account tide and leeway.

Closing a coast in low visibility required particular attention, often using a lead and line. While there were radio beacons, the direction finding equipment in yachts was very primitive with wide errors in rough seas and when the signals

50 sq m Topsy II (ex Dompfaff) in Plymouth Sound in 1940s
Note no guardrails

were weak. There were no GPS systems, echo sounders, radar, computers, or satellites in space for communications. Many Windfalls were very wet boats and plotting on a wet Admiralty sized paper chart using a rolling parallel rule had its moments while using a sextant in a yacht is very different from using one aboard a large ship. The author remembers that the 50 sq m KESTREL had an enormous trailing rotator and a large governor wheel 15 inches or so in diameter, only just clearing the water and clearly purloined from the taffrail of something very much larger. Certainly it was a very comforting sight to watch the wheel rotating steadily at the stern rail, winding down the miles and after a while it was possible to estimate boat speed surprisingly accurately purely on its speed of rotation.

> *Radar reflectors were primitive in those days and it was a quite common but useless practice for a metal frying pan to be hoisted to the wooden masthead in fog.*

Post war safety equipment was very basic, with bulky lifejackets and primitive harnesses, often just a short rope tied on anywhere. Many yachts, including those of the 50 square metre class, had no guard-rails at that time. Even the 100 sq m yachts had no guardrails forward or aft, but simply a short length with four stanchions at the cockpit area. It was very much a question of "one hand for The King (i.e. the ship) and one for yourself", again and again to be heard at safety briefings. Wet weather clothing often comprised a long oilskin coat with a muffler while a sports jacket, with its useful pockets, was practical in kinder conditions. All cooking was done on gimballed paraffin primus stoves, using meths to get things going and of course with no electrics there were no refrigerators or lighting as we know it today. Because the yachts had no engines passages were often longer than today, particularly in light airs, so the cook was a very important member of the crew. Indeed when Commander Aylen advised on the selection of crews for OPERATION HOMEWARD he recommended that the key personnel to be chosen first were the Skipper and the cook (who must have a cast iron stomach), of which perhaps the most important was the cook.

At the end of the war lighthouses and light ships were quickly lit but many buoys were not and there were also mined areas to avoid around UK and the Continental coast. The many different types of buoy in Europe could be confusing and

Sailing clothing was limited. Note life buoy

the standard IALA buoyage system did not come in until the early 1970s. The concept of structured shipping lanes in the Channel had yet to be developed and in addition there was a great deal more coastal shipping than can be seen today.

Launching Merlin's dinghy. No life raft in those days

Thus those sailing these Windfall yachts offshore in the early days were provided with a very real training in basic seamanship, navigation and yacht handling under all conditions. One factor remains changeless over the decades and centuries: the sea.

Qualification of Personnel

Prior to the Second World War the British Services had virtually no system of certification for skippers, mates etc. Very few yachts were owned by the services and for example at the Royal Naval College Dartmouth authorisation to skipper the two yachts there was simply given on the basis of acquired sailing experience. The same applied in the Royal Engineer Yacht Club, a particularly successful organisation. Peter Archer remembers taking TOPSY II offshore in the 1940s, explaining to his fellow young officers in his crew that he had never been out of sight of land before.

With the explosion in offshore sailing by the services following the arrival of the Windfalls, suddenly large numbers of high quality offshore racing and cruising yachts appeared on the scene. The 100 sq m and 50 sq m yachts, 55 feet and 42 feet long respectively, were fast, powerful and had no engine. While in the Solent area there was a bank of experience, further afield there was less. The Windfalls were based at establishments all round the country and there was clearly a need to introduce some system of certification. In the Baltic there remained a considerable fleet so the same requirement arose.

In those days the three British Services were less integrated than today. There was no Ministry of Defence, but an Admiralty, War Office and Air Ministry and this was reflected to some extent down the line. And so it was while all three services had their own Windfalls, even within each service there was no common certification of skippers etc. There was (and is) an Association of Service Yacht Clubs which should perhaps have grasped this nettle but in practice each Regiment, Naval and Air Commands had their own system of qualification, issuing their own certification. Invariably they were based on experience levels and involved no sailing courses or formal examinations.

Some would have said then that certification was not necessary as private owners had none. However the services did (and do) have a duty of care to their personnel and offshore sailing, with its potential dangers, which justified the introduction of a system of authorising skippers and mates with formal certificates. In practice however there was little co-ordinated certification but by the early 1970s things had tightened up and a joint service Services Yacht Proficiency Scheme (SYPS) established. With the rapid expansion of yachting generally, the Royal Yachting Association started taking over the Department of Trade (DoT) training courses and the first RYA Yachtmaster qualifications panel was set up in 1971. The principles of the certification of these qualifications have been copied by sailing organisations world wide.

Many ex Windfall sailors would say that the RYA Yachtmaster scheme arose from the various Windfall qualification schemes, which had before then established courses and used the terms Yachtmaster (Offshore) and Coastal Skipper for years.

Harpy (ex Gunther)
Beken of Cowes

Bill Anderson, the RYA training guru of many years and himself ex Naval, didn't think that to be the case but agreed that there was some connection because so many RYA instructors and staff were ex service anyway, with Windfall experience. What is certain is that the Windfall fleet introduced very large numbers of personnel to offshore sailing, generating the need for a qualification scheme for skippers and crews. This scheme was in being many years before the RYA programme and indeed when the RYA certificates were produced in the 1970s service certificates were simply replaced by the RYA/DoT certificates with no further examination. Since then of course the RYA courses, regarded highly throughout the world, have made an invaluable contribution to offshore sailing safety. Perhaps the Windfall yachts can claim a little credit.

1947–1950

As we have seen, 1946 saw the flood of Windfalls arriving in UK in a series of flotillas from May to October. The majority were sailed back in eight flotillas by Naval crews and assembled in Portsmouth under the authority of the Commander in Chief Portsmouth for allocation to the three services and to bases abroad. In addition about fourteen yachts were sailed to Calshot by RAF crews, some being retained there and the others allocated elsewhere in the three services. In parallel a number were retained in the Baltic to continue the very successful adventure training and racing programmes for the many occupying forces in Germany, principally from the Army. As a sweep up exercise in December 1947 the Admiralty formally issued an Admiralty Fleet Order giving the allocation of yachts and dinghies to all three services at home and abroad.

Already the services were making good use of the Windfall yachts for seamanship training, racing and recreational sailing. As we have seen, the Royal Naval College at Dartmouth received six of the 50 square metre yachts (or more correctly five plus the odd man out HARPY) in the summer of 1946, collecting them from Portsmouth with college crews. Quickly they settled into a pattern of cruising in the leave periods and local racing. In 1947 ORION was entered in the Fastnet Race by the RNSA and was the first Windfall to complete the race while in 1948 the hugely successful first Dartmouth Yacht Rally was organised, with nineteen Windfalls in attendance. At the same time the Army, particularly the Royal Engineer Yacht Club, were quickly on the Windfall scene at Chatham. They were also present in the Solent where there were a number of Naval establishments with yachts based at Portsmouth while the RAF yachts were sailed from RAF Calshot at that time. The Royal Naval cadets at Dartmouth were fortunate in having their yachts on the spot but cadets from Sandhurst and RAF Cranwell had to travel to the Solent area to sail. There was an airstrip at Hamble and Michael English remembers flying there many times with his father (then Flight Lt Nigel English) in an Anson. Nigel was a regular skipper of the 100 sq m SEA LION.

Rapidly the Windfalls were spread around the country. The mighty ORION, the largest of the Windfalls retained for use by the services in UK, was a very

Orion looking aft

popular addition to the Clyde fleet and moored near Garelochhead. David Miller, then aged 10, remembered her enormous size and the careful briefings everyone was given to pay particular attention to operating the heads flushing valves in the right order. Failure to do so could sink the ship as had reputedly happened before in Germany! 50 sq m Windfalls were to be found at stations right round the coast of UK: the Naval Air Command in particular had numerous air stations by the sea and SEA HEXE and SEA SWALLOW were constantly on the move. Most of the yachts were however in the south where there was the largest requirement both to sail abroad or race.

Since time began when two or more yachts are gathered together there is always an urge to race, particularly with young people and the Windfall crews were no exception. Also the yachts were mainly in groups of similar designs such as the square metre classes which led naturally to organised racing. And so it was that very quickly the Windfalls appeared on the racing scene, in the Clyde, East Coast, Solent and West Country areas. And of course, offshore.

Royal Ocean Racing Club Races

1946 saw the first Windfalls entered in the Royal Ocean Racing Club (RORC) racing calendar, the principal UK racing programme, the first Windfall post war participant being GALAHAD from the Royal Naval Engineering College at Plymouth when she came 2nd in the Channel Race then 2nd in the Brixham to Belle Isle Race A Division.

As the Windfalls represented a completely new class of yachts there was considerable discussion about their rating. Lieutenant Peyton-Jones, a very keen offshore sailor and on the staff of the Royal Naval College at Dartmouth at the time, wrote to the Chairman of the Sailing Committee of the Royal Yacht Squadron (RYS) in early 1947 suggesting that there would appear to be no races for which the 50 sq m Windfalls could be entered during Cowes Week. The RYS very quickly and helpfully replied that if it could be guaranteed that at least six

50 sq m yachts could come to the line then the Squadron would see to it that there would be a race for them. Alternately they might be eligible for the small 10–25 ton handicap class, based on Thames tonnage for which there were already three races. In the event the 50 sq m Windfalls came out at 10.47 tons and so from then on they sailed in this class.

Galahad (ex Adler). Royal Naval Engineering College
Beken of Cowes

For the 1947 season there were many Windfall entries in races from the Solent area and in the West Country. The six Windfalls from the Royal Naval College Dartmouth were very successful, sailing over 4000 miles, with 56 starts in the season which resulted in 9 wins (including 2 at Cowes) and 12 seconds.

50 sq m Sea Swallow

GRIFFIN and LEOPARD were particularly successful in a number of races including to La Rochelle. A notable result was achieved by the Royal Engineer Yacht Club (REYC) when their 50 sq m TORCH (ex SEEMOWE) came third out of 40 in the Cowes/Dinard Race. As will be seen in Chapter 9, this year the first post war Fastnet Race took place, with two Windfall entries, ORION of the RNSA and SEAMEW of the REYC.

There was plenty of wind in the Dinard Race of that year, which included a long leg to windward and rough seas. Over forty yachts entered but only thirteen completed the course, of which four were Windfalls, the 50 sq m yachts SEAFALKE I (Royal Marines Eastney), SEEHEXE (Royal Naval Barracks Lee on Solent) and SEAHORSE (Royal Naval Barracks Portsmouth) together with the 60 sq m PLANET (HMS Dryad). However the blue riband of that full Windfall season surely must have gone to the Dartmouth College yacht HARPY for her outstanding performance in the Santander Race. Although one of the smallest yachts in the race she was one of the first round Ushant in a "famous gale" and was the fifth boat to arrive at Santander out of thirty one starters.

RORC Inter Club Points Championship

This important championship was supported by about fifty clubs from UK, Europe and beyond, with results based on the points acquired by yachts from each club. In addition there was a points table for individual yachts. In the 1940's the services, with their Windfalls, were prominent and the Royal Naval Sailing Association (RNSA) won in 1947 and 1948. It was then decided that the RNSA, which as a whole had by far the most Windfalls, should be split into branches for this series. This was done and RNSA (Portsmouth) was still usually a winner until eclipsed by the Royal Engineer Yacht Club in 1952 but still winning four more times before 1960. The RAF Yacht Club, with their new yachts, were twice winners late in the decade, providing a healthy balance between the services. Yet again the Windfalls had played their part in providing a learning ground for many potential offshore sailors.

While there were individual wins for various Windfalls, none of the yachts was ever to win her class in the individual yacht points series. In 1951 when there were 31 yachts in Class 1 (which included twelve Windfalls), five of the first twelve yachts in the series were Windfalls. OVERLORD of the REYC was 5th with MARABU (RNSA Portsmouth) just behind. In Class 2, with 41 yachts, the privately owned 50 sq m REBEL MAID (RNSA Portsmouth) was a very creditable 6th.

The nearest a Windfall got to reaching the top spot in the series was in 1952 when OVERLORD (REYC) was 2nd overall out of 22, an outstanding performance. The other REYC 100 sq m AVALANCHE was 6th, with MARABU (RNSA Portsmouth) again just behind. MARABU continued to race every year, regularly being towards the top of the table but never higher than 5th.

> *Getting to Calshot to join an RAF Windfall (the 50 sq m SPERLING or GOLDAMMER) was always a problem, being inaccessible by public transport. Eventually we developed a pre-arranged routine whereby we would take the Isle of Wight ferry and on nearing Calshot an RAF launch would come alongside to which we were gingerly transferred whilst the ferry maintained course and speed.*
>
> *David Cook.*

Always a very popular venue, Cowes Week attracted many Windfalls from the start. Of course the Solent based yachts took part together with many sailed up from the West Country. GLADEYE, the Household Division 100 sq m was usually well to the fore, prominent on the water and socially.

Dartmouth Yacht Rallies

It was in 1948 that the Royal Naval College Dartmouth put on the very first of the College Yacht Rallies. They sent an invitation to the RNSA at Portsmouth and to Plymouth establishments asking for entries from the 100 sq m and 50 sq m Windfalls hoping for six or so to come. No less than sixteen yachts accepted, of which thirteen reached Dartmouth, for the rally on 12 and 13 June, thus with the College yachts making a total of nineteen Windfalls. Two races were scheduled for the Saturday (with an entry fee of one half-guinea for each race) but within forty minutes of starting fog rolled in reducing the visibility to less than 20 yards. Eleven yachts managed to complete a lap (positions judged from DR tracks on the charts), MARABU being first in the open class while SEA BREEZE led SEA SCAMP in the 50 sq m class. The remaining eight yachts were somehow rounded up and towed into Dartmouth. HARPY (incidentally

50 sq m Martlet (ex Wotan). Royal Naval College Dartmouth

listed as a 60 sq m) had a form of radio and reported that she was "trespassing on the Coastguards' potato patch" and this was sufficient information for her to be located when within a few feet of Coombe Point Rocks. The Sunday races were started but abandoned due to lack of wind. "The Wardroom Officers, the Royal Naval College Dartmouth were At Home at 1930 on Sunday 12 June to masters of all yachts and all officers taking part in the Yacht Rally". Presumably this excluded the naval cadets who formed most of the Dartmouth yacht crews.

Encouraged by the support in 1948, a second rally was organised on 4/5 June 1949, and sixteen Windfalls took part. SEA SCAMP (Royal Marines Plymouth) won the 50 sq m class and PLANET from HMS DRYAD at Portsmouth the open class. The wind was fresh and good sailing enjoyed throughout. Socially too the rally was a great success with a large buffet supper for all crews in the College Wardroom on the Saturday evening, perhaps the first time that the cadets had been inside. They would have been excluded next day when the visitors, College officers and masters were invited by the Commodore for drinks at the Royal Dart Yacht Club.

Through this post war period the Royal Engineer Yacht Club was well to the fore, with OVERLORD, AVALANCHE, their 100 sq m Windfalls and TORCH, 50 sq m. OVERLORD usually had the edge over AVALANCHE and in 1949 took part in every race from the Hook of Holland to La Rochelle.

The tap was now turned on as more and more young servicemen (and some servicewomen) were introduced to offshore sailing. More experience was gained, more skippers qualified and the use of the yachts increased markedly. A pattern of points racing had developed in the Solent while offshore racing and cruising expanded, sharpening boat handling skills (remembering that it was virtually all under sail as there were no engines). Elsewhere round the country the 50 sq m yachts in particular were a much used asset and Windfalls would appear at Clyde Week to the west or Burnham to the east.

A note about flag etiquette at this time, which tended to be somewhat stricter than it is today: the Windfalls were service yachts and they wore their service ensigns or the Blue Ensign when approved. In the case of the Royal Naval Windfalls, some, mainly from the Royal Naval Colleges at Dartmouth and Plymouth, were designated seamanship training craft and fully public funded. These were authorised by the Admiralty to fly the White Ensign but with strict restrictions: it could be flown in a home port or at the start of a major race, but not at Cowes (presumably to limit the heart attacks of the more senior RYS members). Crews had to wear a uniform and be smart. In practice it was

usually just the Dartmouth yachts who used this privilege although as we shall see later the 100 sq m COLLINGWOOD more usually WAL and later MERLIN) was also so authorised for a period.

Merlin's white ensign

And so the 1940s Windfall sailing drew to a close. In a hectic four years hundreds of young people had been introduced to offshore sailing who otherwise would not have been. The yachts, designed for Baltic waters, had nevertheless proved to be seaworthy enough in the more open waters of the Channel and beyond to the Bay of Biscay and round UK. Clearly they were a tremendous asset and their worth to the services was being recognised: seeds were being sown which would lead to sailing further afield.

MERLIN BEEHIVE

The entrance to the old Cherbourg yacht basin in the town was by way of a long narrow north south canal. We were set to leave with a strong wind from the north and as MERLIN had an unserviceable engine she would therefore have to be warped out, bollard by bollard. Stupidly I despatched a less bright crew member to take the bight of the warp ashore with what I thought were clear instructions. He duly put the bight over the first bollard up the canal. Having secured for sea (wrongly including the anchor) we then carefully slipped from the crowded fragile pontoon area and the crew on board heaved away in a seamanlike manner, (there are always ghouls watching furtively when a large yacht is manoeuvring at close quarters, particularly when the Royal Navy's reputation is at stake).

When well on our way our hero on the canal wall picked up the warp and tried to pull us towards him. I bellowed up the canal "LET GO". Pleased to be of help, with an amiable smile he took that literally, lifted the bight off the bollard and threw it into the sea. The effect of twenty-four tons of an out of control Windfall being swept quickly down wind into that small crowded basin was awesome to behold. Somebody kicked the beehive and suddenly there appeared dozens of agitated ghouls all shouting at once and waving fenders. No damage was done but I am ashamed of it still. Author.

CHAPTER 7. 1951–1959. The Green Years

In the early 1950's there began a halcyon period for services Windfall sailing. The service authorities were starting to recognise the value of offshore sailing in encouraging adventure training for young officers and men. In turn more funding was put in to maintain the yachts. The seamanship training Windfalls were fully public funded and small grants were provided towards the running costs of the others, the balance being made up from local grants and by small chartering fees. And so with better sails and some refitting the Windfalls put themselves firmly on the offshore sailing scene. By now the three services entered their yachts in the regular racing series between the Solent sailing clubs and in RORC offshore races. Despite currency restrictions Windfalls were more and more to be seen in France. The Dartmouth Naval College Windfall Rally was firmly established, by now attracting the other services. 1951 saw a further upsurge with the 100 sq m Windfalls coming to the fore with entries from all three services in the Fastnet Race including two sailed over from Kiel.

Seven Windfalls at the start of the 1951 Plymouth to St Malo Race
Associated Newspapers Ltd

The Royal Military Academy Sandhurst had formed a sailing club in November 1946 and were allocated some dinghies, including ex German Olympic Class, to sail on the Thames at Reading and also at Lymington. At that

50 sq m Sea Soldier (ex Seefalke I)
Beken of Cowes

stage THE ROBBE, (soon changed to ROBBE) a 100 sq m Windfall currently undergoing refit, was allocated to the School of Infantry Sailing Club which with RMA Sandhurst had been offered mooring and accommodation facilities by the Royal Lymington Sailing Club. From that connection, as the School of Infantry's finances waned, RMA Sandhurst's interest in ROBBE grew. By 1950 the academy had fully taken on ROBBE for adventure training and there followed a very successful period of use for the next eight years. She was run on a proper upkeep basis, based at Portsmouth, with regular refits. Her cruise logs are full of interest with glimpses of the practicalities of sailing a 100 sq m yacht weighing 25 tons in closed sailing waters with no engine. She regularly sailed in and out of Yarmouth, a small harbour by any standards. An account of her life up to the present day in Norway is in Chapter 12.

OFFICER CADET'S TEETH.
Extract from ROBBE's log.
"Nothing untoward occurred on the week-end cruise. The jib sheet shackle removed Officer Cadet Jones' front teeth."

It was on the 12 June 1951 that a sad but significant event took place three miles east of Start Point. The yacht AMARYLLIS had been at the Royal Naval College Dartmouth since 1927 and used for cadet recreation. Sailed round the world by Lieutenant Mulhauser in the early 1920s, at his death she was lent to the college by his sister with instructions that when she was no longer needed she was to be scuttled. With the coming of the Windfalls after the war AMARYLLIS became surplus to requirements and so in due course Mulhauser's sister's wishes were honoured. The yacht was towed out of harbour, demolition charges placed and the crew taken off. "An arm was dropped, the plunger pressed down and with the Last Post sounding she slipped beneath the waves". The Windfalls had taken up the baton.

By now the College Windfalls were sailing further afield and the next recorded Dartmouth Naval College Yacht Rally was in 1952. There were fifteen Windfalls in attendance including the RAF 50 sq m PIROL for the first time. Passage races were organised from Portsmouth and Plymouth, with WAL and SEA SWALLOW leading their classes. HARPY, the odd man out of the Dartmouth yachts, won the offshore race at Dartmouth, not only winning on corrected time but also took line honours in a fleet which included WAL, the 100 sq m yacht from HMS COLLINGWOOD. Also in 1952 the College had a match against the Royal Military Academy Sandhurst, using four of the College 50 sq Windfalls LEOPARD, MARTLET, GRYPHIS and PEGASUS. In an exciting race Sandhurst beat the Naval College by 5¼ points to 5, adding spice to a spirited party afterwards. Quite understandably the other services always like to beat the Navy on the water and the Army cadet crews did themselves no harm at Sandhurst.

It was in 1952 that a Windfall crossed the Atlantic for the first time, MARABU taking part in the Bermuda Race from Newport Rhode Island (see Chapter 12). This was a tremendous experience for the very young crews who took part and raised the profile of service sailing considerably, adding to the recognition of the value of offshore sailing in leadership and self sufficiency training. It was still over twenty years before the first crewed Whitbread Round the World Race and yet the seeds were now being sown within the services towards longer races amongst young offshore sailors.

With this increased use of Windfalls in racing and adventure training activities, more notice was being taken of them. The down side of this was that a few adverse reports appeared from various quarters about the condition of some of the yachts. These (a minority) were not a good advertisement for the services, particularly for the Royal Navy: poorly maintained hulls and dirty sails projected a bad image. Five Naval Windfalls were dis-masted in the summer of 1953 and a further four masts sprung. As most were Naval yachts, the Admiralty decided that the policy for the maintenance and possible future replacement of the whole of the Admiralty Windfall fleet, in 1953 comprising 27 yachts, should be reviewed and in that year directed that the Royal Naval Sailing Association (RNSA) be tasked to produce a paper with specific proposals. In December the RNSA, having had two yachts independently surveyed as samples, produced its first draft report, limited to 18 Windfalls held by Naval establishments and excluding those already maintained at Admiralty expense at the Naval Colleges for training which were generally in a very good state.

The report is very illuminating and gives a clear statement of the general condition of the yachts while emphasising the huge value of the Windfall yachts to the services. To quote a short passage from the report: "*It is impossible to exaggerate the genuine pleasure and very valuable training which is provided for officers and men by opportunities to sail in these relatively highly developed yachts. This applies particularly to establishments with large ships companies – for example Naval Air Stations in isolated situations. Under the present circumstances of restricted amounts of sea time for so many, the zest and adventure of this type of sailing cannot fail to be of the greatest value to many young ratings, while junior officers are afforded unequalled opportunities for perfecting their seamanship and for making decisions on their own responsibility*".

The report then recommended that the existing scheme of Admiralty ownership and allocation from a central pool to individual establishments, should continue unchanged, that all Naval Windfalls be professionally surveyed and categorised, that an annual maintenance grant be allowed for each yacht and that Admiralty Board approval be sought for a replacement programme for the existing Windfalls. All these recommendations were to come to fruition, eventually leading the way towards a joint service yacht building programme that would not have even been considered were it not for the obvious value of the Windfalls over the post war years.

Seventeen Naval Windfalls were professionally surveyed and it is a reminder of the times to record that the total survey cost to the Admiralty was £254.5s.8d, the average price to survey a 50 sq m yacht being about 10 guineas. A brief statement of the condition of the yachts in 1954 is shown at Appendix 15. It is interesting to read today that in 1954 the 50 sq m DISDAINE had no useful life expectancy while SEA SOLDIER and the 100 sq m WAL (MERLIN) were thought to have three years life. All three are still sailing today (2007) over 50 years later.

By the mid 1950s more modern yachts were coming on to the scene and the Windfalls, while present in numbers, were becoming less successful in the RORC races. The Royal Engineer Yacht Club, always competitive, was quick to invest in new yachts and disposed of their Windfalls in UK. Their 100 sq m AVALANCHE and 50 sq m TORCH were transferred to the REYC at Kiel in 1951 while their remaining 100 sq m OVERLORD went to the Royal Army Service Corps in 1955. The Royal Air Force were not far behind with acquiring new yachts, retaining one or two Windfalls including the 50 sq m SPERLING for recreation.

50 sq m Sea Hexe

Throughout the 1950s the points series in the Solent comprising entries from all the Solent clubs and some from outside, about fifty clubs in all, was hard fought and because of the sheer number of Windfalls in the post war period the services were regularly to the fore. The series had often been won by the Royal Navy under the RNSA umbrella, but in part this was due to the large number of yachts that they could bring to the line because of the number of Naval establishments in the area with Windfalls. After years with the RNSA or the REYC near or at the top of the leader board, the Royal Air Force Yacht Club won the series in 1958, a healthy situation in the overall scheme of things.

1956 was a particularly difficult year with numerous gales and the 50 sq m Windfall SEA HEXE had lost two masts by May. The Channel Race that year was no exception, the weather being so bad that BLOODHOUND, a crack Class 1 yacht with a strong crew, was abandoned off Selsey Bill. The crew were taken off safely by a lifeboat and miraculously BLOODHOUND was not lost as her anchor held, stretching the chain links into a solid rod a section of which may be seen today at the Royal Thames Yacht Club. SEA HEXE, with a crew from Naval Home Air Command was only one of five out of twenty-three to complete the race, winning her class, an outstanding achievement by Robin Foster and his crew.

It was in August 1957 when the first 50 sq m (and probably only to date) Windfall was lost at sea although the loss in bad weather was not due to hull failure but by damage caused when alongside the rescue ship. Five 50 sq m Windfalls from the Britannia Royal Naval College Dartmouth including HAWK were entered for the Channel Race which in those days was Cowes – CH1 Buoy off Cherbourg – Poole Bar Boy – Cowes. GRYPHIS and MARTLET withdrew because of a collision and poor condition respectively. The crew of HAWK for the Channel Race was: Skipper Commander T H P Wilson RN, Captain of one of the Dartmouth Training Squadron ships; Mate Lt Cdr P W Buchanan (Later Vice Admiral Sir Peter) who was one of the Navigating Officers at the Naval College. Crew: Paddy Ryan, John Topp + two others.

Paddy Ryan, then a midshipman at the college, was in HAWK and relates his account of her loss.

Not a good forecast but we set off slowly reducing sail as the Southwesterly increased. If I remember correctly we were down to Storm Jib and heavily reefed main. I remember at one stage I was in the process of tying in reef-points, and hanging over the boom, when the main sheet let go off the cleat and I found myself hanging right out over the side until someone cranked the sheet home again. Yes it was rough, about F 7–8, with one of those happy wind against tide seas that only the Channel enjoys. Most of us were sick, or feeling so, and I remember the cry when asked to do anything of "Hold on a moment while I have a quick puke before doing that" ! Quite suddenly, and without warning, while we were drinking an inappropriate mug of tomato soup there was a loud crack and the mast fell over the side. We managed to lash it alongside for a while, but then eventually slipped it to save further damage. I remember looking at the stump – the break was about 3 foot above the coach roof – and noticing that the inside of the hollow wooden mast was black with 'rot'. As Hawk had that season returned from a full refit in Devonport Dockyard there was discussion how nice it would have been to take a slice from the stump to prove how badly it had been surveyed – but we didn't have a saw!

The Windfalls had no radio – who did in those days – and no engine, so we did not have too many options but were considering a jury rig with the wooden spinnaker pole and boom to get us to Weymouth. But after another cup of tomato soup we suddenly saw a merchant vessel heading down Channel who was going to pass quite close. We fired a red flare and she altered towards us. After some very fine seamanship the 8000 ton ATNA (Swedish?) came alongside us providing a lee. We later discovered that they could only stop and reverse their air-started engines four times before they needed to recharge the starter air bottles, so their alongside had to be carefully judged – which it was. A big sea – perhaps 10 feet – was running despite the lee but we managed to attach a tow round the mast-stump with a lashing between the two? forward cleats. It was an interesting jump and climb up their rope ladder which seemed to go ever upwards. We were very well looked after and given dry clothes while ours were taken to the engine room to dry. Talking of drying, the ship was also 'dry' ! We set off towards Tor Bay with Hawk in tow but it very soon became apparent that she had been 'stove-in' while she was alongside and was rapidly settling. Sadly Hugh Wilson and the Master agreed to cut the tow and she quickly sank taking with her my dinner jacket and an unopened fruit cake! At about 0530 next morning we were transferred to the Brixham pilot boat which landed us at Brixham where RN transport took us back to BRNC. For a short time it had appeared that the ATNA could not spare the time for this transfer and we would have to go on with her to New York. Four young officers rather hoped this might be the case, even if it would have screwed up the rest of the summer leave!

50 sq m Hawk (ex Seesturm)
Beken of Cowes

The maintenance load to keep the Windfalls seaworthy increased and by early 1957 the RNSA was commissioned by the Admiralty to make recommendations for replacing the Britannia Royal Naval College Windfalls with new publicly funded offshore yachts. If nothing else the Windfalls had clearly shown that offshore sailing provided a high training value which needed to be continued. A far cry from the pre Windfall days when the only offshore sail training available to Royal Naval cadets was in loaned yachts. The RNSA carried out a thorough study, obtained proposals from a number of yacht builders and made recommendations remarkably similar to those made by the German staff over twenty years before. The yachts should be fast cruising craft capable of accommodating seven people, sloop rigged and should rate well under the RORC racing rules. They should be of quality, sufficient to last a minimum of 25 years. To enhance the training value no auxiliary engine should be fitted, but provision made for future fitting should it be deemed necessary. And so it was that 1959 saw a major change at the Royal

Naval College Dartmouth when the 50 sq m Windfalls were replaced by five new Morgan Giles yachts, now called Sail Training Craft. These, together with other new yachts acquired within the Navy by grants, fund raising and the sale of some Windfalls, meant that the Navy was once more competitive on the racing scene. The 90 sq m Windfall CAPELLA remained at the College as a popular cruising yacht until 1972.

The decade of the 1950s had seen a huge upsurge in service usage of the Windfalls. The yachts were all in great demand for both sail training, racing and recreation, as can be seen from their logs. They were to be seen throughout northern European waters, by now in Canada, Australia, New Zealand and in the Mediterranean. Windfalls were entered in every Fastnet Race (see Chapter 9) and most RORC races. By late 1959 there were still, however, about twenty Windfalls in UK and more abroad so the story of Windfalls under service ownership continues on to the next decade and beyond.

50 sq m Sperling. RAF Moustaches

CHAPTER 8. 1960 Onwards

The Decline in Service Usage

Although a number of Windfalls had by now been disposed of by the services there were still plenty remaining in the early 1960s although no longer able to come near the top of the leader board in RORC races. Only the Royal Navy's 100 sq m Windfalls took part in the three early 1960s Fastnet Races, with no success. However there was life in the Windfalls yet.

By now as we have seen all three services had acquired new yachts for racing and the UK based Windfalls were more often used for adventure, leadership training and recreation. They continued to provide many young servicemen with offshore experience which as will be seen led to greater things later on. In 1964 MERLIN (RNSA Air Branch) sailed to New York via Lisbon in the Tall Ships Race (see Chapter 12, Some Notable Windfalls) and came back in appalling weather with no damage. Each Tall Ships Race entrant has to include a crew comprising a majority who are young and inexperienced and this was no exception. On that trip the Skipper was an experienced Windfall sailor Sub Lieutenant Leslie Williams while his Mate was Petty Officer Roy Mullender, who got his initial coastal skipper qualification in the 50 sq m Windfall SEA SWALLOW in Scotland, then qualified as an offshore skipper in the 100 sq m MERLIN. Both were to go on to greater things in the sailing world.

Gradually the number of Windfalls in the UK services reduced and by 1965 the Royal Navy had thirteen, MARABU and MERLIN (100 sq m), CAPELLA (90 sq m), the remainder being 50 sq m yachts spread around UK including Scotland, the east and west coasts, the West Country and the Solent. By this time the maintenance, particularly of the 50 sq m Windfalls, was not really keeping pace with their deterioration: sails were not replaced and less funds were available for refits. The yachts tended to be restricted to the Channel and in some cases to inshore areas only. The author remembers taking KESTREL on the Helford to Laberwrach Race in 1967 with nothing more than fresh conditions on the nose yet still water came up almost to the bunks and buckets were required This was a good time for the long sighted to buy a Windfall – for example the 50 sq m DISDAINE was sold by the Admiralty with a sealed bid of a few hundred pounds and she is still sailing today. By 1970 this total was down to just seven. The Army had retained GLADEYE in the Household Division and she was still a regular visitor to Cowes and French ports in particular. At Kiel the Windfalls there, particularly the 100 sq m yachts AVALANCHE, FLAMINGO and KRANICH still thrived with adventurous cruises throughout the Baltic and up the Norwegian coast. Local sailing continued in the 30 sq m fleet up until 1969 when they were at last replaced.

It was at this stage that a major step forward was taken in services offshore adventure training, certainly due to the success of the Windfall usage both in UK and at Kiel over the years. The Ministry of Defence, recognising its value, decided to fund a fleet of nine Nicholson 55 yachts for a Joint Services Sailing Centre based at Portsmouth. This was a major decision which was warmly welcomed and was only possible because of the wide offshore experience now to be found in the services. Men and women were now to go offshore sailing as part of their training and have done so ever since. The programme was given a tremendous launch when it was decided to enter two of the yachts in the 1st Whitbread Round the World Race in 1973.

GENOA LIAISON

"On one Channel crossing in GLADEYE, the skipper reduced sail for the night, lowering the genoa which was laid out on deck, replacing it with the No 2 Jib. It was a calm and warm night. Come the dawn, the skipper ordered "Up genoa", which the crew did smartly. To their astonishment two figures tumbled out of the rising sail, a member of the crew and a young lady cook!"

Coldstream Guards Officer.

50 sq m Sea Feather

Some two years before, Whitbread, the race sponsors approached the Admiralty with a request for support for the race, recognising their access to world wide contacts, communications and secure dockyard facilities. In turn the Admiralty approached the RNSA and in due course by May 1972 it was decided that the RNSA would take over running of the race, which they did very successfully. The icing was on the cake when ADVENTURE, the RN Nicholson 55, came first in three of the four legs and was second round the world overall, the winner being the Mexican yacht SAYULA 11. The Mate of the 3rd leg and Skipper of the 4th was Chief Petty Officer Roy Mullender of the MERLIN trip to New York mentioned above. Like so many, Roy's very successful sailing career all started with his experiences in the Windfalls.

100 sq m Gladeye (ex Reiher)
Beken of Cowes

The last naval 50 sq m Windfall in service was SEA FEATHER, still at HMS Ganges in 1975 and in 1976 the 100 sq m yachts MERLIN and MARABU completed their final season with the Royal Navy. While Windfall sailing continued at Kiel, the curtain on the UK service Windfalls was finally drawn when GLADEYE, the 100 sq m of the Household Brigade Yacht Club, was sold in 1979 after 32 years continuous service. To servicemen in UK that was the end of the Windfalls. Little were they to know that a completely new era had already started for some of the Windfall fleet and now more would follow which would last into the next century as we shall see.

The Upsurge in Civilian Usage

As the requirement for Windfalls in the services declined they were not scrapped but put on the Admiralty Disposals Lists and sold by sealed tender to the highest bidder. In the event the successful applicants were mainly civilian but a few servicemen were fortunate. All the purchasers knew that the yachts had beautiful lines but not all realised the work involved to maintain them. Thus for a period many Windfalls disappeared from sight but there were notable exceptions such as the 100 sq m OVERLORD, the 50 sq m yachts SEA OTTER (now SEEOTTER) and MARTLET (later MARLETTA) which were quickly back on the scene. OVERLORD, established first by Tony Venables as the Overlord Sailing Club when he bought her in 1961, was continued under the auspices of the Offshore Cruising Club in 1963 and has continued to this day. (See Chapter

Overlord and Sea Scamp in the Solent 2007
Martin Hayden

50 sq m Seeotter at speed 1990s

12, Some Notable Windfalls). She still is a classic example of how a large classic yacht can be maintained and continuously sailed by sheer good organisation. The 100 sq m yachts in particular would need an individual owner to have very deep pockets and so the most common and practical form of ownership today lies in a properly run syndicate.

Following this slump in Windfall numbers, gradually more and more reappeared, particularly with the increase in awareness of them as classic yachts. This was helped considerably by the foundation in December 1995 of the Association of Square Metre Yachts (German Rules) by Tony Venables and John Kapp, leaders of the syndicates of OVERLORD and SEA SCAMP together with MARABU/KESTREL respectively. This drew together some twenty-five owners of Windfalls and formed a valuable communications link with newsletters and social events for a period. Further, this association became connected with the European Classic Yacht Union (ECYU) and remained in being for some years. Later, when the organisation of each of these four yachts formed into separate syndicates or clubs, the Association of Square Metre Yacht Clubs was formed for a time. Clive Brown, a previous Commodore and leading light of the SEA SCAMP syndicate for a long period, is currently trying to revitalise more communication between owners and syndicates. As can be seen from Chapter 13 (So where are they today?) a surprising number of Windfalls have been refurbished and may be seen round the country and far beyond.

Rather like classic cars, there was a time when Windfalls could be bought for a song. Gradually, as the years have gone on, they have actually appreciated considerably and a Windfall in good condition today can sell surprisingly well because of its rarity and sheer quality. Today a 50 sq m Windfall can sell for up to £30,000, a far cry from the sales from the Admiralty Disposal Lists with successful bids of under £1000.

The activities of a number of individual surviving Windfalls since they left service hands are to be seen in Chapter 12 (Some Notable Windfalls) and Chapter 13 (So Where are they Today). The chapters clearly show the amount of sheer effort that owners and groups have put in to keep their Windfalls seaworthy. In some cases almost superhuman dedication has been required to recover a yacht which has deteriorated almost too far. Sometimes initial stripping might involve first a little replanking, gradually leading in cascade fashion into timber and iron rib replacement, etc etc. A number of Windfalls, including ZEEAREND (ex WAL), PINTA (Ex BRUNHILDE), NORDWIND, SEA SOLDIER (ex SEEFALKE I), and HILTGUND have been totally rebuilt to "Museum Standard" and today are universally admired at the Classic Boat gatherings. Then there are others, and good examples include OVERLORD, SEA SCAMP, FLAMINGO and DISDAINE which have been given first class regular maintenance year after year to keep them at sea today in top condition and for the foreseeable future. Then there are others such as MARABU, SEEOTTER and KESTREL as it were waiting in the wings for their next stage.

While the 100 sq m and to a lesser extent the 50 sq m yachts have been more readily traceable the same cannot be said for the 30 sq m Windfalls. Being smaller (although still 32 feet LOA) in some cases they deteriorated more quickly and in other just have passed out of sight. SUNA (ex AEGIR) and PHOENIX (ex BUKANIER) and AVALON (ex ALEMANNE) are still sailing but little is known about the majority of what was a large fleet. Hopefully this book will generate more information on their whereabouts.

ADMIRAL'S HEADS

The Admiral, a large and somewhat humourless man, was on board SEA OTTER and like any mortal needed to visit the heads. They were in a tiny cramped compartment forward and it was necessary for him to take his trousers down before turning to sit down. In so doing he completely demolished the flimsy temporary partition fitted for privacy, exposing his white posterior like a Belisha Beacon in the gloom to the startled crew. I always felt that my promotion prospects were thereafter somewhat reduced.

Peter Richardson

CHAPTER 9. The Fastnet Races

In the years after the war the Fastnet Race was one of the three premier races in the world, the others of similar length being the Bermuda Race and the new Sydney to Hobart Race. It was decades before the concept of trans ocean and round the world racing and at the time these races were the pinnacle of offshore racing: only those who had completed the Fastnet Race could be considered for membership of the Royal Ocean Racing Club. Naturally, now that the services had the use of the Windfall fleet, adventurous eyes turned towards the Fastnet with its challenges including the likelihood of August gales. As we have seen, there were far fewer safety facilities such as life rafts or radios in those days: how they would have survived the freak conditions of the 1979 Fastnet storm is pure conjecture. Based on other very rough conditions that they experienced over the years the hulls would probably have stood up to it although the hollow wooden masts would have been a weakness.

ASTA was entered in the 1937 Fastnet Race by the Kriegsmarine under the Marine Regatta Verein scheme whereby German naval officers paid two marks a month towards yacht maintenance. Later taken as a Windfall she could thus be said to be the first of the yachts, albeit under German ownership, to be entered for this classic event. For the next race in 1939 NORDWIND, a newly built 60 ton yawl entered by the Kriegsmarine, achieved line honours in that race in a time not beaten for 26 years. This was the principal achievement in that race of any Windfall yacht (although not then truly a Windfall, being under German ownership) over their lifetime.

The first race after the war was in 1947 in which there were just two Windfalls – the 150 sq m ORION of the RNSA and the 50 sq m wrongly named SEAMEW (which should have been SEEMOWE), later TORCH, of the Royal Engineer Yacht Club. Only ORION finished, although near the end of the fleet, but staking her place in the history of the fleet by being the first Windfall (i.e. being under British ownership) to complete the Fastnet course.

Eight Windfalls were entered in 1949, six in Class 2. This represented 35% of the overall fleet, equivalent to over a hundred Windfalls today, which gives some idea of their numerical impact on offshore sailing in UK at that time. In light airs six did not finish but SEA OTTER of HMS Vernon clung on to come 4th out of 20 in Class 2, a very creditable performance. Nevertheless the entries were an indication of the increasing enthusiasm in serious offshore racing. A notable entrant was the Royal Naval Engineering College Windfall GALAHAD, skippered by Nigel (later Rear Admiral) Malim and listed as not having finished although in fact she did so, taking over 11 days and 8 hours. Mike Jones, a crew member, recalled that they had taken 8 days to reach the rock and had run out of water so they motored into Baltimore to replenish and to report to the college because some of the crew were due to start the Santander Race in the other college yacht. Their cable was received by the Duty Staff Officer at Plymouth "GALAHAD ARRIVED BALTIMORE. STOP" which caused a certain amount of consternation.

1951 was a classic race and keenly contested by the strong Windfall entries. AEGIR X (150 sq m) and LIVELY (125 sq m) were entered from the British Kiel Yacht Club and KRANICH (100 sq m) had also been sailed over from Kiel for the race, entered by the Royal Air Force. MARABU (HMS Hornet) and OVERLORD (Royal Engineer Yacht Club) were also 100 sq m entrants so

60 ton yawl Orion. The first Windfall to complete a Fastnet Race
Beken of Cowes

together they enjoyed a true inter service race. 38% of Class 1 entries were Windfalls.

There was an impressive international line up for the race which started in appalling conditions with winds of up to 40 knots against a strong tide. In the Solent a crack American entry MALABAR VIII lost its mast, AEGIR X had to retire and several yachts including LIVELY sheltered under Hurst Castle. OVERLORD had to temporarily leave the race to get a new backstay runner block while others pushed on, some retiring to Cherbourg. At this stage the skipper of BLOODHOUND (not a Windfall) smashed several ribs and the tiller, but was lashed to his bunk and they continued the whole race under emergency steering, finally coming 4th overall. LIVELY split her mainsail and retired to Weymouth. Later the weather eased and the modern lightweight yachts

50 sq m Sea Otter. Achieved the best Fastnet Race result of any Windfall
Beken of Cowes

won the day. It is of note that all three 100 sq m Windfalls completed the course when there were 13 retirements out of 29 entrants. MARABU, KRANICH and OVERLORD finished 5th, 8th and 9th respectively out of a class of 13 mainly more modern yachts, so it was a very creditable showing. Already elegant, the 100 sq m design again proved to be very durable.

The weather was appalling for the 1957 race with a force 9 on the nose for the start and Capt John Illingworth RN in his MYTH of MALHAM (who was to win Class 2) suggested to the organisers that they change the course to leave the Isle of Wight to starboard because of the hazards of the Needles Channel in a severe gale. His suggestion was not agreed by the committee (although it is now an accepted alternative in the event of extreme weather) and for the only time no Windfall completed the course, five having started including three 100 sq m yachts. For the next three Fastnet Races there were three large Windfalls in each race, all 100 sq m except for NORDWIND in 1953, now under private ownership. A sprinkling of 50 sq ms took part in that period, the last being SEA WRAITH in 1959 although she did not finish. A highlight in 1955 was the performance of GLADEYE, the Household Brigade 100 sq m skippered by Robert Boscawen (Coldstream Guards). Although beaten on corrected time by MARABU, GLADEYE won the Jolie Brise Cup for the first yacht home in "A" Division and the Hong Kong Cup for the winner of "A" Division. MARABU, skippered by Rupert Thorpe (Commodore of the RNVR Sailing Club) did well to win the Inter-services Club's Cup.

From 1959 the Windfall performance dropped off against more up to date opposition. MARABU was the mainstay with her eight successive Fastnets and appropriately she brought down the curtain on Windfall Fastnet entries in 1965, coming 29th out of 33 in Class 1. By this all time entries in Class 1 were more than all the post war total fleet. Over the years there were 37 Windfall entries in what was still one of the three classic international offshore races. Thus several hundred servicemen were introduced to this premier race in a period when it would otherwise not have been possible. A complete list of all Windfall entrants in the Fastnet Races together with how they finished is attached at Appendix 16.

Sea Wraith. The last 50 sq m Windfall to enter a Fastnet Race
Beken of Cowes

Chapter 10. The Baltic Scene

Although so far the focus has been on Windfall activity in UK, it must be remembered that in parallel sailing in Windfalls was continuing full ahead in the Baltic. Indeed it is still continuing today with the 100 sq m Windfall FLAMINGO in use for training after 60 years of virtually continuous use. She is the last remaining Windfall sailed by the British services.

We have seen in Chapter 3 that the old Kieler Yacht Club was taken over in 1945 and renamed the British Kiel Yacht Club (BKYC) for the next six years. This became the principal base for recreational and later adventure training for British forces serving in Germany which has continued to this day. In addition there were many clubs and centres where the yachts and smaller craft were located, ranging from Flensburg and Schleswig to the north, down through the coast including Eckernforde to Kiel. South of the Kiel Canal some yachts were to be found in the Cuxhaven and Bremerhaven areas. Royal Navy and Army sailing became focussed on the Kiel area while the RAF occupying forces had some of the yachts including some 100 sq m and 50 sq m craft based near Schleswig. Further afield, in addition to their yachts, the Army in particular had small craft on the various local lakes, in particular to the south at Plon, where there was and still is a German naval enlisted mans' training school.

Throughout 1945 there had been a massive number of Windfalls including very many small craft in use by the services in the Baltic, with many cruises in company and ad hoc races between the many clubs. This was a turbulent time and with the value of hindsight it is remarkable that a good measure of control of the yachts was established so quickly, leading to clear ideas for their future use. The decision by the Admiralty and Treasury to bring the majority of yachts and smaller craft to UK was naturally resented by many units of the occupying forces, who needed some for their own use. This was represented and more craft were left in Germany as a result.

Reference has been made in Chapter 3 of the impact that the ex German Naval Officer Bruno Splieth had on the Windfall scene at Kiel from September 1945 for the next 40 years. He was "the rock on which the British Kiel Yacht Club was founded" and a pivotal example of the goodwill generated by the Windfall fleet.

As we have seen 1946 saw the great exodus of many yachts from the Baltic to the UK in OPERATION HOMEWARD and to a smaller extent OPERATION SALLYPORT. There was tremendous activity throughout that year, not only in preparing the yachts for sailing but also coping with the large groups of personnel sent over from England to form crews and sail them back. There were huge numbers of occupying forces so on top of all that there was recreation sailing to organise and fit in somehow. A club cruising race was held early in the year and a rough system of handicaps established for the wide variety of yachts, ranging from the 150 sq m class such as JACUNDA down to 6 metre yachts. Following on from its success in 1945 a Kiel Week was held during August and Danish, Norwegian and Dutch guests took part. There were many weekend cruises into the Baltic, particularly to Denmark and inter club races continued, by now on a more structured basis. There was more cooperation between the various service units – for example at the end of that year the British Air Forces of Occupation laid up their yachts at the British Kiel Yacht Club.

By early 1947 the situation had steadied down somewhat and long term plans made for a more sustainable future. By the start of the season virtually all of the Windfalls destined for UK and the Commonwealth had left the Baltic and it was in that year that the Baltic offshore sailors began to sail further afield. The first of three cruises to Sweden that year was made by Major Blomfield who was on the Chief Royal Engineer's staff at Kiel, (reported to have been in the 100 sq m Windfall KONIGIN, but other reports state that KONIGIN was returned to a private claimant in 1946, so possibly Blomfield may have taken another 100 sq m as FLAMINGO and KRANICH were at Kiel at the time) failing to reach Stockholm because of light winds but the pattern of using long leave periods was set. Around the south Baltic area club regattas were re-established, by now including some German civilians. And so the experiences of Windfall sailing in the Baltic expanded. In 1948 the 180 sq m yacht ASGARD went to Oslo as part of the Norwegian King's birthday celebrations, again skippered by Major Blomfield.

It became clear that some of the more exotic yachts, fun though they were to sail, were impractical to keep because of the problems of maintenance. Clearly the most rugged yachts of similar class design were the ones to keep in the longer term. While most of the 50 sq m yachts had been sailed to UK, a few were kept at Kiel (ANNELIESE, KUCKKUCK, SEEFORELLE and JOSTE). Of the nine 100 sq m Windfalls only FLAMINGO and KRANICH remained but AVALANCHE was to return in due course.

There remained a core of large yachts, JACUNDA, AEGIR X and LIVELY, all 28 tons and described as 150 sq m although some would dispute the classification. LIVELY was also described as a 125 sq m and had been a particular favourite of Rear Admiral Baillie-Grohman during his time as Senior Naval Officer Schleswig Holstein.

During the next few years a number of important events occurred in the area. By the end of the 1951 season financial pressures arose in the BKYC and it was decided to return the club house to its former owners i.e. the Kieler Yacht Club. The BKYC then moved to Stickenhorn where it has remained ever since. To quote from the history of the British Kiel Yacht Club, "*At the same time, all the privately owned yachts that had been requisitioned in the post-war period were returned to their owners, in good condition and with a full inventory. The owners were each paid a charter fee for the period that their boats had been requisitioned*". Honour had been satisfied.

In the winter of 1950/51 the British Kiel Yacht Club, hitherto for officers only,

100 sq m Windfalls Flamingo and Kranich at Kiel in the 1980s

amalgamated with the other ranks Victory Sailing Club, which resulted in the emphasis being placed on cruising more than racing. It was at that time that the 30 sq m yachts, hitherto distributed round various Baltic clubs, were centralised at Kiel as a class. Most of the older large and miscellaneous yachts were phased out and, just as in UK, the fleet thereafter consisted mainly of 100 sq m, 50 sq m and 30 sq m Windfalls until in turn new yachts came along. By 1951 the 100 sq m AVALANCHE had been returned to the Kiel branch of the REYC from the REYC in UK, joining FLAMINGO and KRANICH for training, longer range cruises and races. Remarkably these three 100 sq m Windfalls, together with the smaller 42 ft ketch RASMUS, were to continue at Kiel for more than forty years.

It was in 1956 that one Captain Stan Townsend arrived and he was to have a far reaching impact on the way ahead at Kiel which was to continue to this day, establishing more formal sail training courses for all ranks. He also proposed upgrading the 30 sq m fleet but this had to be rejected on cost grounds in relation to their useful life remaining. However from his initiatives the value of sailing for service training (as opposed to recreation only) in yachts was appreciated and in turn this eventually led to the Treasury allowing money from the sale of ageing Baltic Windfalls to be used towards replacement yachts for training purposes there. In the 1960's Maj General John Woollett, as both Chief Engineer and Commodore of the BKYC, and his staff finally reached formal agreement on this principle. This process was happening in UK at the time (the Royal Naval College Windfalls were completely replaced by new Admiralty funded yachts in 1959) but it only happened because it was realised what training benefits were to be gained from the yachts. All the time more and more servicemen were learning about the benefits to be gained in sailing craft of all sizes in terms of self reliance, adventure and fun.

The story of the further development of the sailing facilities at Kiel belongs elsewhere, but suffice to say that over decades they have been expanded, fleets of modern yachts purchased, adventure training and RYA courses established. Membership has widened to include all ranks and families. Thousands of young service personnel had been introduced to offshore sailing. All this stemmed from the Windfall yachts back in 1945: indeed a historic connection has been maintained throughout by three Windfalls being retained at Kiel for many years, FLAMINGO, KRANICH and RASMUS, although now only FLAMINGO remains.

The Baltic Today

Recently we sailed to Germany mostly over the waters that the Windfalls took the other way in 1946. We had modern equipment, good sails and an engine. For a while we went inside the Frisian Islands, unlike the Windfalls, into waters that were only just deep enough, able to do this because of modern aids and magnificent Dutch and German charts. There were modern marinas, clearly marked channels and the usual first class weather forecasts.

Returning another time we came through the Dutch canals, following the track of a number of Windfalls, remembering Scotty in Haalem with SEETAUBE on a wild run ashore or the mastless WOTAN being towed to Amsterdam. How very different our trips were compared to 1946, then a different world in leaking wooden yachts with no engines, radios, life rafts, proper safety equipment or guard-rails, quite apart from the dangers of minefields, wrecks and inadequate weather forecasts. But, like today although perhaps more memorable, still fun and never forgotten.

We since flew out to Germany initially above the same track that the various destroyers took carrying the Naval Windfall crews from Portsmouth to Kiel sixty years ago. Below us too the RAF Sunderland flying boats of Coastal Command had taken their yacht crews from Calshot to Schleswig and Cuxhaven. Passing over the Channel we thought of those Windfalls sailing to England, a few cruising easily, others battling to windward, some through appalling weather. Meanwhile PLUTO was plodding to and fro ferrying more and more small craft and the 30 sq m Windfalls.

In no time we were in Kiel, now a modern city and rebuilt today after its almost total destruction in the war. It was very moving to check into the elegant Kieler Yacht Club Hotel, built in 1887 before quickly becoming the Imperial Yacht Club and the scene of the very start of the Windfall story in May 1945 as the British Kiel Yacht Club. This was where it all began: where Colonel Fryer, the Deputy Chief Engineer of 8 Corps, had started it all. In front of the club today is the same piled marina that was established there for the 1936 Olympic Games.

We were made very welcome at the club, in particular by Captain Klaus Kinast FGN and the 88-year-old Life Commodore Otto Schlenzka, the widely respected father of German sailing. He joined the German Navy in 1936, from the start was a keen sailor in the Star class and was on the short list for the German team in the 1936 Olympics but could not be released after the Spanish war. After a very active World War 2 at sea (including seeing the HOOD blow up and being in the cruiser PRINCE EUGEN for the famous Channel dash) Otto was at the Naval Academy at Flensburg in 1945. He became very successful in the Star class and moved into sailing administration, becoming Chief Race Officer in the Olympics at Kiel in 1972 and advisor to other nations including Korea at their Games. He is only the 4th Commodore of the Kieler Yacht Club, the first being Kaiser Wilhelm II.

The club facade while mostly still the same as in 1887 and 1945, has been

Otto Schlenzka. Commodore of the Kieler Yacht Club

changed in character by a modern extension forwards and an accommodation block to the left built in the 1960s for the 1972 Olympics.

Internally the club, while still elegant, has a modernised layout suited to the needs of a first class hotel and the premier German yacht club. Nevertheless one was always conscious that these were the very rooms where Scotty and his friends used the chandeliers as trapezes at yet another wild party before setting off in SEETAUBE and five other Windfalls for England.

Then up Kiel Fiord to be warmly welcomed at the combined Kiel Training Centre and British Kiel Yacht Club, still providing superb facilities for young servicemen as in those momentous days in 1945. Almost unbelievably, in the old seaplane hangars for her winter refit, lay FLAMINGO, the 100 sq m Windfall which has been in service at Kiel continuously since then. Now very much the Old Maid of the club, she nevertheless enables groups of ten to cruise year after year in the Baltic waters exactly as those veterans of

Kieler Yacht Club today

WW2 did in the early club days. She holds the record for longevity in service use by a Windfall by a very long chalk and is a credit to the enthusiasm of all those who maintain her. In the next yard was the Windfall RASMUS, a club yacht for nearly 50 years before being sold to a private owner in 1992.

Kiel Training Centre and British Kiel Yacht Club

The yachts used by the Kiel Training Centre are owned by the British Kiel Yacht Club who charter them out, replacing the fleet every three years. This magnificent modern facility only exists because of those early days of the Windfall fleet. The staff of under forty are a mixture of service, civilian, British and German and it was a pleasure to visit such a friendly and cohesive unit. Manfred Esser, a German

100 sq m Flamingo
Beken of Cowes

who has worked on the yachts at the centre for 30 years, told the author of a little story handed down: soon after the war a Windfall sailed to Denmark with a British crew and one German, probably the skipper. The latter had no foul weather clothing so the crew clubbed together and bought him some, which made a profound impression, remembered to this day sixty years later. Yet another legacy of goodwill that the Windfalls generated. The Splieth Regatta is still held annually.

Eckenforde, the compact town which included the headquarters of 30 Assault Unit, where NORDWIND lay at the jetty under the watchful eye of Commander Aylen, is little changed today except for an extended harbour front. Schleswig has expanded and it was apparent that the Schlei Fiord would have been ideal for the operation of seaplanes such as the Sunderland. Nearby there are airfields such as at Jagel which were taken over by the occupying air forces. While some of the ex Luftwaffe yachts were collected from the Schleswig region it is not clear where they were based: Schleswig itself is about 22 miles from the sea and the Schlei is narrow, which means that large yachts would need a long tow in unfavourable winds.

The German Naval Academy at Murwick, Flensburg is essentially the same, with upgraded facilities and supported now by the three masted training ship GORCH FOCH, built in 1958. In front of the Academy there are still the pens with rows of naval yachts, as there were in 1936, bringing to mind the saying "What goes around comes around". So many years have gone by since Admiral Raeder and others of the Kreigsmarine recognised the value of offshore sailing for young personnel, a principle continued to this day and through the Windfalls transmitted to a very wide audience indeed.

Chapter 11. Windfalls Abroad

Once the majority of Windfalls had reached UK and the dust settled it was agreed that in addition to the occupying forces in Germany there were other servicemen serving abroad to be considered including those of the Commonwealth countries. At that time there were massive movements of personnel and equipment by sea to and from the Far East and so it was relatively simple to transport the smaller craft to where they were wanted.

KIEL

The Kiel area was of course where the Windfall story began and the turbulent period there in 1945 and 1946 has already been described in Chapters 3 and 4. Since the formation of the British Kiel Yacht Club in 1945 the club has formed the centre for British services sailing in North Germany which has continued to this day where in addition to the many modern craft the 100 sq m Windfall FLAMINGO is still in service. See Chapter 10 The Baltic Scene.

MALTA

By late 1946 the 30 sq m Windfalls GOTE and SEEJUNGFER had been received "In excellent condition", together with PLUM (25 sq m) and MAX, both "In poor condition and should only be used for picnics". Two STARS were also received

30 sq m Gernet off Malta

in time for the 1947 season, followed that year by GERNET, another 30 sq m. Gradually more 30 sq m yachts, PHOENIX, SALUKI and SUNA were added, and then in 1954 the RAF Windfalls FLANDERN and FALKLAND came. More STARS were added and so in the early 1950's Malta had a number of flourishing sailing clubs of all three services and shore staffs, with a core offshore fleet of 30 sq m Windfalls. ROSANNA, a 50 sq m Windfall belonging to the Gunners, came to Malta from Tripoli in 1950. She had perhaps the longest trip of any Windfall, being loaded in UK on to a Royal Fleet Auxiliary ship which was diverted from the Mediterranean and sailed round the world for some months before being offloaded. When craned into the water she was observed by Colonel Woodford Norman-Walker, Colonel of the Gunners there, to sink immediately to the bottom of the harbour as she had opened up so much. She was left submerged for a while and in due course her timbers took up, but no doubt she was as wet a boat as any thereafter.

In 1951 there was a 30 sq m class race Round the Island, won by Colonel Garrett in SALUKI. Four Windfalls took part in the race to Syracuse in Sicily, which was won by Commander Cowburn in GERNET. At the end of this season the redoubtable Captain John Illingworth RN arrived in Malta, having previously won both the first Sydney Hobart Race and two Fastnet Races in his own yacht. He immediately became a driving force to get the Windfalls more race worthy and there followed a high period in offshore sailing from Malta. By 1952 there were six Windfalls entered in the Syracuse Trophy Race, including the 50 sq m ROSANNA. After a thrilling race with most yachts leading at some stage, ANGELA, skippered by Captain Illingworth won with SALUKI and SUNA only minutes behind after 60 miles.

It was in that year that Captain Illingworth in ANGELA achieved the greatest success in the Mediterranean of any Windfall, winning what was then regarded as the Championship of the Mediterranean. This took the form of two offshore races, from Cannes to Cagliari in Sardinia (340 miles) then the second race from there to Palermo, a further 240 miles. To get to Cannes from Malta Captain Illingworth had to sail the 30 sq m Windfall about 500 miles to windward in up to gale force headwinds, itself a very impressive achievement. There were twenty-five entrants from six nations for the Championship, the Italians being particularly strong and traditional winners. The first race was in heavy conditions and won by an Italian Class 1 yacht, but ANGELA came second and won her class. The second race was in mainly light airs with ANGELA again winning her class and overall Championship. As was reported at the time "It all goes to show what can be done with a Windfall".

A Malta Windfall highlight came in 1954 when the island was visited by HM The Queen and the Duke of Edinburgh in the brand new Royal Yacht BRITANNIA. Orders from the Commander in Chief included the entry "0840. Windfall yachts sail past and salute". The whole Mediterranean fleet was in two columns either side of BRITANNIA approaching Malta when the seven 30 sq m yachts FLANDERN, SUNA, GERNET, PHOENIX, FALKLAND, SALUKI and ANGELA sailed in line between them, only a cable from BRITANNIA. A loyal message was hoisted and later Prince Philip sent a signal "I enjoyed seeing the yachts this morning: they looked very smart. Thank you for your message. Admiral RNSA".

AUSTRALIA

Following the success of Captain Illingworth in winning the first Sydney Hobart Race in 1947 under the RNSA burgee, the Australian Navy was keen to get a yacht suitable to enter. In 1948 the Windfalls SCHWALBE II (30 sq m) and SWANDER WITT (18 sq m) were brought to Australia in HMAS KANIMBLA but of course were too small for the big race. Later it was heard that the Windfall HELGOLAND, a fine 30 ton yawl was now surplus to the Admiralty's requirements and in the early 1950s strong efforts were made to get her. Letters went to and fro between the different departments and with the Admiralty in London which make painful reading. Eventually it was a case of faint hearts not winning a fair lady. The delays in the Australian Ministry with concerns about upkeep costs effectively lost the bid for the yacht and HELGOLAND, now called PICKLE, went to the Canadian Navy instead where she was sailed very successfully for years.

Despite the setback with HELGOLAND, the Royal Australian Navy made very good use of the smaller Windfalls. SCHWALBE II, built in 1937 by Abeking and Rasmussen, regarded as the best of the Windfall builders, was well to the fore racing in Sydney for many years in Division 4. In 1952, now with a new rig, she had a number of wins and was the leading yacht in her division.

When The Queen and the Prince Philip came to Sydney on 3rd February 1954 for the first ever visit of a reigning Monarch to Australia it was described in the Australian Branch report of the RNSA journal as "the most memorable day in the history of Australia". The Royal Yacht GOTHIC anchored in Sydney Harbour to a cacophony of sound and the Royal party transferred to the Royal barge before coming down a long line of ships and yachts

30 sq m Schwalbe II in Australia

on the way to the shore. There was SCHWALBE II, with her RNSA burgee at her masthead and Prince Philip (who was Admiral of the Association) drew The Queen's attention to it. To quote the RNSA Australian Branch Secretary "I shall never forget the thrill we all received when his Royal Highness recognised the RNSA burgee at our masthead".

It was in 1956, with SCHWALBE II now in the 3rd Division, that she won the points series and also in that year won her first race in Australia skippered by a lady, Mrs J Stuart-Duff. She was still being sailed by the Navy in 1959 but there are no reports of her activities after that.

30 ton yawl Pickle (ex Helgoland). She went to Canada
Beken of Cowes

The Australian Navy enjoyed good relations with the RNSA in England. They were already branch members of the RNSA and in 1951 the Central Committee in London invited the RAN to provide a permanent member, which was done from the RAN Liaison Staff. Recognising the training advantages of offshore sailing initiated by Windfall sailing, the Australian Naval Board purchased the 33 ft sloop TAM O'SHANTER for the Naval College in 1955. And so it was that the cadets were at last able to crew their own yacht in the Sydney to Hobart races.

CANADA

The Windfall PICKLE (ex HELGOLAND), a handsome 30 ton yawl designed by the legendary Henry Gruber and built in 1937 by Burmester, a powerful combination that also produced the Windfalls NORDWIND and BORKUM (CAPELLA). She was taken over by the Canadian Navy in 1953, having first been offered to the Australian Navy and was similar to the 100 sq m class but slightly larger. She was the sister ship of ROLAND VON BREMEN, winner of the 1936 Transatlantic Race. Canada was also allocated two 50 sq m Windfalls GLILSE and TUNA, again based at Halifax.

PICKLE was used extensively for seamanship training based at Halifax, Nova Scotia and in 1956 she sailed 600 miles south to Newport to take part successfully in The Bermuda Race, following on from the Windfall MARABU in 1952. She continued to give good service as HMCS PICKLE until 1979, when it was reported that she was abandoned at Halifax, Nova Scotia. In 1984 she was renamed PICKLE and "attempts made to salvage her". However, like so many Windfall stories, the yachts never actually can be confirmed as having been scrapped until there is a death certificate. For PICKLE was indeed resurrected and today as HELGOLAND I has been completely reconstructed over the past four years with new mahogany planking fixed to the steel ribs and the whole hull epoxy coated. In late 2006 she was to be seen, in mint condition in Gaspe, Peninsular, Quebec, up for sale as a Classic boat.

HONG KONG

In January 1947 8 STAR Windfalls were reported to be sailing, having been brought out in the aircraft carrier HMS INDOMITABLE. They lay at moorings at the Hong Kong Yacht Club. During 1947 several lost their masts but new ones were quickly made locally.

SINGAPORE

4 STARS arrived in late 1946 (probably also in HMS INDOMITABLE) and were soon racing. An attempt was made to form a STAR boat club but it was found that they were better maintained by individual units. It was reported that the Army boat PROCYON was the best and RIGEL the worst.

NEW ZEALAND

The New Zealand Navy was very keen to get hold of a Windfall and in due course the Admiralty (with letters signed by one Lieutenant Commander Erroll Bruce RN) offered LEUCHTAFER, listed as a 30 sq m yacht although like so many pieces in the Windfall jigsaw records are often in error for she was in fact a 50 sq m. Although also described in New Zealand sailing journals as being a 30 sq m her dimensions and tonnage are clearly shown on the shipping manifesto and

50 sq m Tangaika (ex Leuchtafer) in Auckland Harbour

are identical to those of a 50 sq m. There then came the question as to who would pay for the passage of the yacht to New Zealand, which neither the Admiralty nor the New Zealand authorities would agree to do. Eventually the RNSA, in the spirit of encouraging sailing, offered to pay the required £100 themselves and so it was that she was shipped in the "New Zealand Star", arriving in Auckland on 26 July 1949. The whole transfer was carried out in a "can do" spirit with complications of customs, insurance, dock charges and other administration sorted out later.

The first question was what her name should be changed to. One idea was GLOWORM, the English translation of her German name but eventually a Commander Washbourne suggested TANGAIKA, the Maori term for Spoil of War and this was immediately agreed.

For the next decade she was put to very good use within the New Zealand Navy although as new yachts came on the scene she was not particularly successful on the racing circuit. This was not for the want of trying and at one point she was re-rigged, enabling her to carry a larger mainsail, working jib, jib topsail, masthead genoa and a masthead parachute spinnaker. Her leading light for a period was Lieutenant Commander E B Davies and with his crew became well known in the racing scene. However TANGAIKA's main forte was cruising and she was much in demand for trips in the Haurai Gulf, mainly to the Kawau and Waiheke Islands, the WRNZNS being well represented. The RNZN, while not agreeing to pay the transport charges for her shipment to New Zealand, nevertheless were very supportive of the yacht and provided dockyard assistance for slipping the boat every winter and funds for essential repairs. Administration came under the Commanding Officer of HMNZNS PHILOMEL, the naval barracks at Auckland. Painting and general maintenance was provided by volunteer labour and modest fees charged for recreational sailing which formed a fund to cover minor improvements and insurance.

When she was laid up in 1956 it was found that she was uneconomical to repair. By July 1957 she was declared surplus to requirements and finally on 19 October of that year was auctioned off, being sold to a Mr G Palmer. And so it was that in December 1958 the Navy Office in Wellington wrote to the RNSA to state that TANGAIKA was no longer economically viable and she had been disposed of (incidentally this was the year that the Royal Naval College Dartmouth 50 sq m Windfalls were replaced). Now in private hands she was redecked and her topsides raised by one plank. At this stage she was bought by two brothers, Bruce and Ian Gilchrist, who gutted her and found problems. To cut a long story short they much strengthened her by replacing several planks, sheathing the yacht with two layers of Philippine Kauri and covering the whole with glass fibre.

GIBRALTAR

Two 30 sq m Windfalls EASE and AEGIR were allocated to the combined services Gibraltar in late 1946. Little is known of their sailing but as late as 1978 the author took one, across to Morocco with a crew from the 4th HMS ARK

ROYAL returning across the Straights in fog. Her condition then was marginal, but apart from the fog it was still fun.

BERMUDA

One STAR and one OLYMPIC were allocated to Bermuda in 1947.

THE RECENT YEARS

We have seen above the distribution of some of the Windfalls abroad soon after the 2nd World War: of course the majority had already come abroad, having left their native Germany. In addition since then of course a number have spread further afield and indeed in SEEFALKE I (SEA SOLDIER)'s case, back from UK to Germany. Others, disposed of from the British Kiel Yacht Club, have remained in Germany (RASMUS, the 100 sq m AVALANCHE and KRANICH, the 50 sq m ANNELIESE, KUCKUCK, SEEFORELLE, JOSTE and a number of smaller Windfalls).

NORDWIND, ROBBE, WAL (MERLIN now ZEEAREND), BRUNHILDE (now PINTA), SEEFALKE II (SEA EAGLE) are now showing the Windfall flag in different countries, mostly as true Classic Boats. They are much admired and talked about as all wooden boats are, keeping the name Windfall very much alive today.

CHAPTER 12. Some Notable Windfalls

All windfalls could be said to be notable, certainly in the eyes of those who sailed them. Many have since disappeared into oblivion, others are known to be around but their whereabouts are unknown. Here are a few examples of Windfalls that in their own way have made their mark over the decades.

NORDWIND

A 60 ton, 85 ft yawl, NORDWIND was the most powerful of all the Windfall fleet and has retained her German name throughout her history. Designed by the famous Henry Gruber, she was built for the Kriegsmarine by Yacht-und Bootswerft Burmester in Bremen in 1939 and was regularly sailed by Karl Donitz, later Commander in Chief of the Kriegsmarine, as skipper. In 1939 she took line honours in the Fastnet Race in a record time of 3 days 16 hours and 28 minutes which was not beaten for 26 years.

We have seen Commander Aylen's account in Chapter 4 of his taking over NORDWIND and running her throughout 1945. He was very keen that she should be sailed to UK that year but it was not until May 1946 that he finally sailed her to Portsmouth. Thus the British services enjoyed just one year's sailing in her, for Commander (later Rear Admiral) Aylen and his crews never to be forgotten. In that year out of touch officials in the Admiralty looked at various ways that she might be used, not understanding that she was an offshore sailing yacht with no engine, not a steam yacht suitable for foreign embassy work or a cargo ship.

In due course NORDWIND was sold and first appeared on the Lloyds Register in 1949 as owned by Squadron Leader K J Nalson. She was then sold to Lord H W Astor who was to own her for about 15 years. He campaigned her in RORC races, winning the Cowes to Dinard Race in 1950 but she was only raced intermittently thereafter and used mainly for cruising. One account stated that she was then to be sold for the value of her lead keel, before being refurbished by Camper and Nicholson. This has not been verified but what is certain is that she was acquired by a Dutchman and fully reconditioned in 1979. By 1986 Ugo Baravalle, an Italian, bought her before she finally returned to German ownership in April 2000. Dr Hans Albrecht became her new owner and had her taken under tow to Alcudia, Mallorca. Then began a massive complete rebuild which was to take 4 years, involving 26 craftsmen from 14 nations. She was stripped of her planking, leaving her steel skeleton which was sandblasted and renewed where applicable. The work was split into three areas – the exterior was rebuilt by boat builders headed by a Swedish shipwright Jesper Olsen, the interior by an Argentinean cabinet maker Freddy Connon while the mechanical, plumbing and electrical work completed by a team led by a Scottish engineer Brian Bird.

The result has been a wonderful success. She joined the Mediterranean circuit in August 2004 and took part in the major regattas in the south of France and Italy. In early 2005 she went to the Caribbean for charter work and has subsequently rotated between there and the Mediterranean, taking part in the Transatlantic Challenge Race in 2005 and 2006. Restored with the aim of retaining as many features as possible from 1939, she is a true Windfall of which both Admiral Donitz and Rear Admiral Aylen would have been very proud. A photograph of NORDWIND is shown in Chapter 3.

MARABU

MARABU (100 square metres) has been perhaps the most successful of all the Windfall yachts to date (although this would not be agreed by OVERLORD and MERLIN), certainly during her time in the Royal Navy. Like NORDWIND, she retained her German name throughout. She was built by a leading boat builder Abeking and Rasmussen for the Luftwaffe in 1935 and until 1939 was used by them for navigation and seamanship training in the Baltic. Like many Windfalls, she was reputed to have been the personal yacht of a senior officer, but while there is no foundation for that, there was a specially large bunk up for'd and Goering was a large man ...

In 1945 she was gathered into the fleet of Windfalls in the Kiel area and later in 1946 became a favourite of the redoubtable Commander Martyn Sherwood, Senior Officer (yachts) at Kiel and was sailed with him as skipper back to UK in the last batch of Windfalls in September 1946. Allocated by the naval authorities to HMS Hornet at Portsmouth she immediately entered into the offshore racing circuit sailed by the Coastal Forces Sailing Club, affiliated to the RNSA. In 1947 she was second in her class in the Round the Island Race. Many successes followed and she was first in her class many times. She competed in eight Fastnet Races, more than any other Windfall.

In the winter of 1951/1952 she was examined by Captain John Illingworth RN, one of the leading offshore yachtsmen of the day, twice winner of the Fastnet Trophy and one instigator (also winner) of the first Sydney–Hobart Race. He recommended that MARABU's fore triangle be increased by moving the forestay forward three feet. This would enable larger genoas and spinnakers to be set which in turn would provide an improved performance with a reduction in weather helm.

Secondly, in view of a forthcoming Trans Atlantic trip, he recommended that a coach roof be installed. This latter proposal was a source of considerable debate. The purists realised that installation would detract from the lovely flowing lines of the 100 metre yacht but there were considerable practical advantages to be gained and Captain Illingworth's proposal won the day. Since then the coach roof has proved its worth, giving shelter to those on deck, providing additional space and altogether a drier boat.

In 1952, skippered by Sam Brooks, MARABU sailed the Atlantic to Newport, north of New York, took part in the Bermuda Race and then raced back to UK. This was a highly successful venture and although overshadowed by the outstanding racing performance of another small RNSA yacht SAMUEL PEPYS

100 sq m Marabu. The Royal Navy's most successful Windfall
Beken of Cowes

(which had gone out to America in a merchant ship), she made many friends and truly showed the flag throughout. On this trip she encountered bad weather and had many adventures, not the least of which was when Stoker Mechanic Hogan was washed overboard in mid ocean. It was mainly due to the heroic action of Chief Shipwright Flux, who managed to climb to the lower cross trees and spot Hogan some distance away, that the man was saved. Even then, with Hogan's exhaustion combined with a high sea state the rescue was only achieved with great difficulty. Years later, in a poignant twist of fate Sam Brooks himself was flipped overboard in mid Atlantic but not recovered.

At this stage, like virtually all the 100 square metre Windfalls, MARABU was sloop rigged with tiller steering (see pictures above). It was in the winter of 1952–1953 that the third stage of Captain Illingworth's

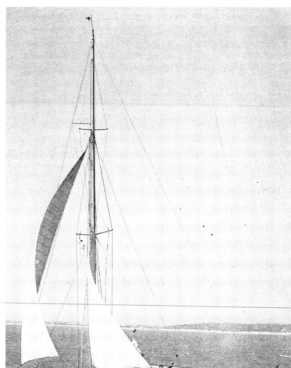

Marabu leaving Portsmouth for America. March 1952

recommendations was completed – the insertion of a mizzen mast and consequent wheel steering which was carried out at the Camper and Nicholson yard in Portsmouth. She has remained as a ketch ever since. A small engine was fitted for the first time.

MARABU was the Royal Naval entry in the first Tall Ships Race (skipper Lt Cdr Geoffrey Wardle) in 1956 from Torbay to Lisbon. This hugely successful event has continued to this day, initially always with a Windfall in attendance, sometimes several. She continued to be cruised and raced by naval crews throughout the 1960s, her last Fastnet Race being in 1965. In the early 1970's the Joint Service Sailing Centre was established at HORNET with nine powerful Nicholson 55 yachts and MARABU's days as a seamanship training yacht were numbered. She became uneconomic and with the Navy's other 100 square metre yacht MERLIN was sold in 1977. Hundreds of naval personnel had benefited from the recreation, adventurous and seamanship training provided in MARABU.

It was then that the third and equally successful phase of MARABU's life began and indeed has continued until recently. In 1978 she was bought by John Kapp, a very keen sailor and since 1970 one of the skippers of the ex Army 100 square metre Windfall OVERLORD, then based in the Hamble. John formed a syndicate and based MARABU at Brighton Marina where they had good support from the RYA in running courses for Yachtmasters and Yacht Master Instructors.

Marabu keel removal 1987

One feature of owning a Windfall and running it on a sustained basis of long distance cruising and racing is the sheer hard work of winter maintenance. It is clear from John Kapp's records that, bearing in mind that MARABU was about 40 years old when he acquired her, that no stone was unturned to keep the hull and rigging in good order. Notes like "keel bolts withdrawn", "some planks replaced" etc were routine entries, involving an enormous amount of effort. In 1987 the whole keel was dropped, a major operation for such a heavy yacht.

John had himself passed the RYA Yachtmaster Examiner examination in 1982 and thereafter ran about six courses a year. In parallel MARABU took part in most of the Tall Ships Races, to Portugal and the Baltic in alternate years. These races are for young people, thus continuing the adventurous sailing pattern. And so it has been that in over 70 years with German, Naval and civilian crews MARABU has been providing the best possible service for which she was built.

In 2004 MARABU was sold to Christopher Dean and she is now lying at Ipswich.

OVERLORD

OVERLORD (ex PELIKAN), 100 sq m is almost unique amongst the Windfalls, certainly amongst her class, in that (like FLAMINGO at Kiel) she has been in continuous use since she was acquired by the occupying forces in 1945. Even before that she was the first of the 100 sq m yachts that were to become Windfalls to take part in a pre war offshore race – the 1937 Heligoland Race. It could be argued therefore that she is the most successful of all of them, although this would not be agreed by MARABU and MERLIN.

She was built by Abeking and Rasmussen as PELIKAN in 1936 for the Luftwaffe and was one of four Windfall yachts offered to the Royal Engineer Yacht Club (REYC) in 1946, becoming based at Marchwood, a Royal Engineers Port Construction Unit in the upper reaches of Southampton Water. The REYC was always a very competitive club and she was quickly into the RORC offshore racing programme, taking 3rd place in the 1949 Channel Points Series and winning a number of class events. Under the REYC pennant OVERLORD took part in two Fastnet Races, several North Sea Races and a series of races from the North Sea to La Rochelle.

In the early 1950's the REYC ordered new yachts and the requirement for their Windfalls for racing declined. Two (AVALANCHE and TORCH) were transferred to the REYC branch based at the British Kiel Yacht Club in 1951 and 1953 respectively, while OVERLORD transferred to the Royal Army Service Corps (RASC) Yacht Club in May 1955.

Tony Venables

It was at this point that Tony Venables entered the Windfall scene and uniquely has remained there to this day. Tony, a Captain in the RASC who had considerable inshore sailing and water transport experience, was asked "if he had webbed feet" and giving a reply to the affirmative was asked if he would like to take over the running of OVERLORD, subject to a trial cruise to Cherbourg. This was achieved satisfactorily although at Cherbourg it was Tony's first berthing of the yacht which like most Windfalls had no engine. Curiously, Tony's Colonel, thinking it the correct thing to do, decided that formal respects should be paid to the rather bemused Port Admiral before returning to the Solent. And so began one of the longest personal associations with any yacht in the entire Windfall fleet. Tony took over the running of OVERLORD from that time in 1955 which was to continue in one form or another for the next 50 years.

The yacht was put on to the strength of the Water Transport Training Company at Freshwater, Isle of Wight and based at Yarmouth for the first year. She was used to run War Office courses for officers joining the Water Transport units, giving them basic experience of the sea in variable conditions. At that time the Company already had another Windfall, the 30 sq m SACHSE. 1956 was a busy time for Tony: having had his honeymoon aboard OVERLORD early in the year he then went off to the Suez operation before returning to the Water Transport Company. At that time refits were carried out at Gunwharf,

Overlord. The last 100 sq m Windfall still sailing in UK
Beken of Cowes

just inside Portsmouth Harbour. It was in 1956 that an engine was fitted for the first time and Tony enjoyed towing the naval 100 sq m Windfall MARABU back to her mooring occasionally. From then on until 1959 OVERLORD, under the RASCYC pennant, was mainly used for cruising in the Channel with the odd race together with War Office courses.

It was in 1960 that she lost her wooden mast and it was decided that she be put up for disposal. And so it was that when she was put up for sale in 1961 Tony, who had by now just left the service, decided to bid for her. It was a very bold decision and very much a leap into the unknown. The bid process was complicated, separated into hull and equipment in two lots and in the end Tony succeeded with a bid of £600 for the hull and £150 for the engine, heads, cooker, sails, dinghy and bunk cushions. As Tony recalled fifty years later, his idea was to refit the yacht, run her for two years and sell her. It was not to turn out that way.

Illingworth and Primrose helped design a new rig, converting her from fractional to masthead rig and with a shorter boom. Highfield levers were removed, replaced by tackles. And so it was that in 1962 she set off on a series of cruises in the Channel on a charter basis with friends and acquaintances. Such was the apparent enthusiasm that Tony agreed to form an OVERLORD Sailing Club if 30 members could be found but while words were supportive in practice there was a poor response to actually paying up. It was then that Tony took a far reaching initiative, proposing free cruises for those who introduced new members and also a club tie. He had to order a minimum of six dozen (an outlay of £80, a huge amount then) and yet that was the key to solving the difficulty. Members poured in and by the first AGM in November there were sixty members and the club firmly established, in due course changing its name to the Offshore Cruising Club, the name retained to this day.

From then on the yacht was chartered for cruises in the Channel and to France until in 1969 Tony sold OVERLORD to the club syndicate members, where she has remained ever since with Tony as Admiral. That year saw the first trip to the Baltic, followed by trips to Spain, changing crews there. So the pattern continued for a decade, with Tony as a principal skipper, until in 1982 she was entered in the Tall Ships Race for the Falmouth to Lisbon leg. She then went to the Mediterranean which proved hugely popular, wintering in Turkey. This was regularly repeated, refitting in alternate winters in Majorca, Turkey and Sicily, returning to UK each subsequent year. As with MARABU, some of the refits were extensive, always with the long term aim of keeping the yacht in good order for the foreseeable future. Such was the impact of the Offshore Cruising Club activities on the wooden yacht sailing scene that Tony Venables was nominated as a finalist in the 1988 Nautical Silk Cut Yachtsman of the Year Award in recognition of his "Services to Square Metre Yachts".

In the past decade OVERLORD has sailed further afield to the Azores, Turkey, Scotland, Scandinavia, the Baltic and countless places in between. She is the very model of how a 100 sq m Windfall can be run when no individual deep pockets are available. The syndicate has a large and enthusiastic membership, and recently the author was welcomed for a brief sail . . .

We joined OVERLORD on a Spring morning (2007), welcomed in the sunshine with a cup of tea and warm smiles. It was immediately apparent that she, the last of the 100 sq m Windfalls still sailing in UK, is a much loved yacht. Years of the combination of keen volunteer help and proper investment for maintenance have clearly paid off and she is a credit to her owners and indeed builders. From tip to toe she is the epitome of a classic boat with all that that implies, turning heads wherever she goes.

For the author it was the first time that I had sailed a 100 sq m Windfall since MERLIN (ex WAL) in 1970: what a difference, and yet despite the metal mast some endearing features remain. Even though she is now a cruising yacht, OVERLORD has no roller headsail reefing. So the old, simple yet infallible method of reducing sail by changing the many headsails remains, with its many hanks off and on to the single forestay. The tiller seemed to resemble that of a Thames Barge and must feel like one on a broad reach in fresh conditions. However on that Sunday morning in a light breeze she was a pleasure to handle – rather like a quiet carthorse, knowing all the while that she could be a handful if she wasn't respected. With 23 tons and a long keel she didn't exactly turn on a sixpence but was manoeuvrable enough in the crowded Solent.

Overlord chart table today

However it was below decks that the biggest changes became obvious. Within the cosy mahogany woodwork and white paint there are fresh white easy clean surfaces, a new heads forward and a modern stainless steel galley. There in the spacious navigational area are all the gismos that yachtsmen seem to want these days (although interestingly no radar), including an electronic map which when it is working must make navigation child's play. And so we came back to the jetty, now under a powerful engine, having stowed our Terylene sails and put out our plastic fenders. It had been a brief but very meaningful interlude. OVERLORD is in very good hands indeed.

MERLIN

MERLIN (ex WAL), with her long, unusual and happy history, is the subject of the cover photograph of this book. After a period in the doldrums she has now emerged newly refurbished as currently the very best of all the 100 square metre Windfalls (although this may not be agreed by OVERLORD and MARABU), under her fifth name, ZEEAREND.

To begin at the beginning, she was built for the Kriegsmarine (German Navy) in 1938 by the excellent builder Burmester on the River Weser, under the name WAL and was used by the Kriegsmarine until the war. In 1945 she was duly taken over by the occupying forces at the German Naval Academy near Flensburg and, having been built for the German government, was classified as a reparation, i.e. a Windfall in common with all the other government owned yachts. Here a complication arose, because one Herr Petersen, a German (although some documents say Swedish) civilian said that he owned the yacht, having bought it from the Kriegsmarine, and had the papers to prove it. In the turmoil of the times, Lieutenant Peter Richardson RN, who worked for Commander Martyn Sherwood (Yachts Officer), took the yacht anyway and explained to Herr Petersen that he should represent his case to the Control Commission. Staffed by the Civil Service, the Commission had been established to administer amongst many other things the vexed question of who owned what. They wore khaki uniforms with green flashes and were known to the occupying forces as the Green Lizards.

WAL was sailed to UK in June 1946 by Lieutenant Commander Hayward RNVR and six Fleet Air Arm officers from Lee on Solent, arriving at Whale Island in Portsmouth. Three months later Martyn Sherwood was sent for by the Commander-in-Chief Portsmouth and told that the Green Lizards had upheld Herr Petersen's claim and that WAL was to be returned to him.

Unexpectedly the upshot was a happy one for all parties. Martyn Sherwood and Peter Richardson put forward the idea that the problem could be solved if they could find another 100 sq m yacht for Herr Petersen so that the Royal Navy could keep WAL. They went to Rensburg where they found that the Army there had little use for a beautifully varnished 100 sq m yacht KONIGIN but desperately needed dinghies for use on the lakes. In due course a deal was done and several Sharpies, Stars and a Dragon were found and the Army was happy. KONIGIN was given to Herr Petersen and he was happy (as Peter said "That the British had done the decent thing") and the Royal Navy was happy to retain WAL.

Meanwhile a very keen group of officers and ratings from HMS COLLINGWOOD, the Royal Naval Electrical School at Portsmouth, led by Lt E Spalding, had taken the yacht in hand, given her a quick mini refit and immediately set off on a summer cruise. And so it was that WAL remained with HMS COLLINGWOOD, formally being allocated on the 3rd of August and berthed at HMS HORNET, a shore establishment at Gosport. A Collingwood Cruising Club was formed which was to be a model of its kind, recognising

100 sq m Merlin (ex Wal)

from the start that offshore sailing was for officers and ratings alike and the constitution of the club's committee reflected this. A practice of properly writing up WAL's logs was maintained which were in due course finely bound and may been seen to this day at the RNSA Central office in Gosport. If only more Windfalls had such good early records.

It so happened that at that time the Admiralty decreed that only shore establishments with a ship in commission could use the term HMS. So that the large shore establishment could be HMS COLLINGWOOD, WAL was designated to be a ship in commission and duly flew the White Ensign for a period, to the disapproval of some members of the Royal Yacht Squadron who until then virtually alone shared that exclusive privilege. On the subject of flags, WAL in her time flew the German Ensign, the White Ensign, the Red Ensign and the Blue Ensign with the Admiralty anchor.

For some curious reason with her new status WAL was named COLLINGWOOD for a period, but this only seems to have been referred to in Admiralty correspondence for in her log books she remained firmly as WAL for the next ten years. It was not long before she was formally renamed WAL, although in later Admiralty correspondence she was called either WAL or COLLINGWOOD at the same time for a while. She had a most successful decade at HMS COLLINGWOOD, being mainly used for adventure training in the Channel although in the mid fifties she did return to the RORC offshore racing programme with great enthusiasm but little practical success. By that time many more newer yachts were on the water.

In 1957 she was transferred to the Naval Air Command and renamed MERLIN. At about this time she was given a major refit and fitted with a coach roof similar to that fitted to MARABU, a major improvement when going to windward although not pleasing to the purist in comparison to her previous lines. A 22 hp Lister engine was fitted – she had not had an engine since the original one was removed 15 years before.

Although now twenty-five years old, this was the period when she raised her profile in Royal Naval sailing, being entered for more RORC races including the 1963 Fastnet. She then set out on her most ambitious service trip – the 1964 Tall Ships Race first to Lisbon then to Bermuda, followed by a more casual race to New York. The skipper throughout was Sub Lieutenant Leslie Williams, ably assisted as First Mate by Petty Officer Roy Mullender, later a Whitbread Round the World Race skipper and Naval Sailing Coach. Mullender had more on his shoulders than he bargained for because Williams was severely ill with blood poisoning throughout most of the Lisbon–Bermuda leg. He was the only one who knew how to use a sextant so Mullender had much to mug up on including the procedures for burial at sea. The majority of the crew often were young trainees, as required by the Tall Ships rules, but in any event of the usual age for service adventure training sailing.

The log of that voyage makes interesting reading, with delightful gaps. Before sailing from Plymouth they were supplied with "eighteen 4.5 gallon jerricans and an extra 100 gallons were made up from wine containers with taps".

Unfortunately there is no mention what was in these containers – not wine but was it water or (perhaps more likely) fuel? As an aside, with water, diesel, petrol, paraffin and meths all stowed in containers it is a sensible precaution to label them. It also makes the coffee taste better.

The trip was a huge success, with many friends made from the other ships and in Lisbon, Bermuda, New York and New England. Being a Royal Naval ship particular attention was shown to her and she was swamped with visitors including the Governor of Bermuda, Lord Martonmere. While in New York all the crews were given a ticker tape parade down Broadway, an experience of a lifetime. MERLIN then sailed up to Newport and, awash with yet more overwhelming hospitality, finally sailed for home. This was no passage cruise as they experienced gale force winds for 19 days out of the 23. In particular it worsened still in the latter stages and they were under bare poles with trailing warps for a period. She arrived in UK battered but undamaged: once again a Windfall had truly shown its mettle in both weathering major storms and showing the flag.

Merlin's crew at Portsmouth after her 23 day run from New York. Roy Mullender, back row, third from left. Skipper Leslie Williams with cap by mast

In common with other service branches, the Naval Air Command now bought new yachts and the Windfalls dropped out of the offshore racing scene. MERLIN continued to have good use as an adventure training yacht but in time the maintenance costs rose. Finally, together with the other naval 100 sq m MARABU, she was sold by the Admiralty in 1977.

Wal cabin 1940s

For MERLIN there followed a long period in the Doldrums. She first went to the Mediterranean under private charter then had a succession of owners, gradually going downhill, ending up rotting in a Norfolk field at East Dereham. Then she was at her lowest ebb, seemingly never to recover. At that point in 1987 she was discovered and bought by businessmen Malcolm Parish and Robin Whitby and they formed the Merlin Restoration Group, with the aim of setting up a scheme aimed at rehabilitating drug addicts in Docklands. She was put into the Walter Cooke yard at Maldon in Essex and a restoration programme started. Anglia Windows put up some funds for specific items in sponsorship but later withdrew their support when financial problems arose. MERLIN was to have been on loan to the London based Discovery Docklands Trust but gradually it became evident that with the lack of sponsorship the owners had bitten off more than they could chew, a very familiar story in the world of restoring classic boats.

Eventually she was sold and moved to a London site. And so for the second time by 1991 MERLIN sank towards oblivion, seemingly never to recover. It was at this time that the media dubbed her "Hitler's Yacht" which was patently untrue as were many other claims to fame.

And then, out of the blue, like Cinderella, she eventually found her Fairy Prince, which every decaying classic boat dreams of. A Dutchman, Leo Aarens (or rather his wife) spotted a small advertisement "for restoration" in a British magazine. Leo drove to

Zeearend (ex Wal) cabin today

100 sq m Zeearend (ex Wal, Collingwood and Merlin) today
Robert Mens

London and the upshot was that MERLIN was brought over to Holland into the yard of A & van G Sachtbouw in Rotterdam for a full inspection. Fortunately she passed well enough for a full restoration to be possible, retaining her classic proportions. And so it was that MERLIN, now with her fifth name ZEEAREND (Sea Eagle), over some considerable time has now been rebuilt completely. Her coach roof has been removed to return her to her old flowing lines, the steel frames partially replaced and epoxy glued strips inserted between the hull planking, the whole being covered by glass fibre. She is now cutter rigged with a small staysail and has a split cockpit to allow for a mainsail sheet track. As a result she now has wheel steering, with a spoked wooden wheel in the after cockpit section. Interestingly, like the original 100 sq m yachts, she has no guard-rails but removable stanchions can be fitted to meet current racing regulations. Internally she is beautifully fitted out with mahogany and white paintwork. MERLIN (ex WAL and now ZEEAREND) has proved by example that given sufficient resources and determination anything is possible.

ROBBE

A 100 sq m Windfall, ROBBE was sailed to England in July 1946 by a Naval crew skippered by Lt Cdr Fryer as part of OPERATION HOMEWARD. She had previously been reported as racing in the Baltic against MARABU in July so presumably that was part of her work up phase. When she arrived in UK she was allocated to the School of Infantry where she remained for four years.

Like many organisations running large wooden yachts before and since, the school found running ROBBE difficult. She required considerable maintenance and the expenses involved were not justified by the usage. In parallel with this the first meeting of the Royal Military Academy Sandhurst (RMAS) Sailing Club had been held in November 1946 and over the years had been sailing dinghies (including the ex German Olympic class) since then. The club also became affiliated to the Royal Lymington Yacht Club and so members came to develop an interest in offshore sailing. In turn RMA Sandhurst chartered ROBBE for several week-ends and also Cowes Week in 1949 and so it was when it was suggested that RMA Sandhurst take her over in January 1950 the offer was readily accepted.

There followed a hectic period of refitting, helped by the Royal Marines who had previously been preparing her for her return to the Admiralty. In a very short time the mast was removed (and condemned), her internal layout changed, dry rot eliminated and the saloon cabin top rebuilt. The inside was repainted and somehow the mast was recovered by re-glueing and fitted with strengthening hoops. When Majors Carver, Ross, Glennie and Captain Parry arrived to sail her on 2nd April she was in the water with no mast. They slipped and anti-fouled her, enamelled her topsides and using a crane from HMS RESOURCE installed and rigged the mast. Sails were bent on and on 11 April she was ready at Gunwharf to take on the first RMAS crew. It was a lesson in what could be achieved with sheer determination, one which was to be repeated with many Windfalls in the ensuing years.

There began a halcyon period for the yacht, mainly due to the keenness of various officers on the staff at Sandhurst who quickly got things on to a proper footing. Initially she was sailed in the Solent, itself a good work up area as she had no engine, with Yarmouth a favourite watering hole. During this first year cruises were extended along the Channel and by October she had visited a number of Channel Island and French ports. She was continuously sailed every week-end and throughout the main college leave periods, with officer cadets initially as crew then taking on more and more duties. As well as sailing the yacht they all worked hard at maintenance. It was a good start.

In 1951, now refitted and with a new mast, ROBBE expanded her horizons and took part in the RORC Harwich to The Hook of Holland Race, beating her REYC sister ship OVERLORD and winning her class. There followed more cruises punctuated by Cowes Week and the Round the Island Race before heading round Ushant to Concarneau and Benodet. On her return trip the yacht experienced her first real gale when she was under a small stay sail only for 24 hours. Bad weather continued for the rest of the season and a further cruise round Ushant had to be curtailed. However ROBBE had stood up to the weather very well and was generally considered a dry ship. She was in continuous use until 28 October having in the season given experience to 143 officer cadets, 4 lecturers and 21 officers. Throughout the winter of 1951/52 working parties from RMAS

100 sq m Robbe
Beken of Cowes

further improved the yacht's interior including the removal of a ton of useless engine.

By now ROBBE was a familiar yacht in the Windfall scene and a very popular attraction of the RMAS Sailing Club which was to grow to over 320 officer cadet members. The pattern of sailing seasons continued, with short and long cruises, occasional races including the sociable Round the Island Race. Maintenance work by cadets in the winter months was also beneficial in their getting to know the yacht and learning about the complications and planning requirements for a successful refit. As well as routine scraping, painting etc there were always new jobs such as changing the internal layout, improving the pumping arrangements etc. In 1956 a rather ugly but effective small dog house was installed, providing shelter but not adding to the yacht's lines.

Because she provided sailing for large different crews of officer cadets, her programme was not really suitable for the RORC racing programme and she was never to compete in a Fastnet Race. However her utilisation remained very high and her programme was a model of how to use and maintain a large Windfall, providing offshore sailing experience for large numbers of young people.

ROBBE'S DINGHY

Coming through the Needles our (clinker) dinghy towed astern became full of water. It became a burden so we slipped it with a note on board addressed to the finder. In due course it was found on the Shingles Bank and returned to us.

In her penultimate season with the RMAS, ROBBE made banner headlines by going "missing" for nearly two days. In fact she had sailed from Omonville to clear a potential onshore gale, was unable to reach Cherbourg due to the tide, then sailed round the Casquets and to the south of Guernsey but was unable to beat up the Little Russell to St Peter Port. Thereafter, with deteriorating conditions she had little option but to look for sea room and head across the Channel, hove to trailing warps, reaching Falmouth with no damage to yacht or crew. At the same time LEOPARD, a Royal Naval College Dartmouth 50 sq m Windfall had lost her sails and been towed in. Yet again the media had inflamed the situation, causing some unnecessary worry to next of kin. In fact few new lessons were learnt, again stressing the importance of sound equipment and the fact that yachts cannot be run "on the cheap".

In 1958 it was decided, thanks to a generous Nuffield Grant, to provide a new yacht for the RMAS and WISH STREAM was launched in 1959. Yet again a Windfall had shown that offshore sailing provided worthwhile training value in terms of adventure and leadership, justifying investment in a new yacht. 1958 was ROBBE's last season with the RMAS and as no other Service club was interested in her she was sold by the Admiralty Disposals Branch in June 1959.

About 1500 officer cadets had sailed in her. During her time with the RMAS from 1950 to 1958 very good logs were kept. These were leather bound and are now held at the Academy library at Sandhurst.

Her new life as a civilian yacht started in Belsize Boatyard in 1960, moving on to a Michael Wulf Purdue in 1961 and then Hedley and Paddie King in 1964 before being acquired by Stephen Penny in 1966. It was probably at this stage that the whole interior was gutted and frames and fastenings renewed. Unfortunately brass bolts were used instead of the original gunmetal ones and electrolysis caused severe problems. Eventually the bolts were gradually replaced using stainless steel each time the yacht was ashore.

Now came a very unusual phase for a Windfall because Stephen and his family including three children lived aboard ROBBE for three or four years in England then two more in Norway before moving ashore to a house outside Bergen. Meanwhile he had a large doghouse built and the cockpit moved aft to make more room for his family. The yacht was then used as a summer house and sailed along the Norwegian coast. It was in 1988 that the present owner, Bjarne Engen, bought her and for the next six years sailed her up and down the

Norwegian coast, very often alone for up to three weeks at a time. In those years he had many experiences of bad weather when alone and he writes laconically of various adventures, such as being unable to get the mainsail down, in a rising gale, of the yacht heeling so much that water came in through the engine ports, leaving him without an engine for entering narrow fiords etc. This is the first known reference to a 100 sq m Windfall being sailed single handed.

Robbe in the Norwegian fjords

In January 1994 a severe storm, described locally as a hurricane, damaged Robbe and sank another larger yacht nearby. Over a period of time Bjarne built his own slipway leading into a large building that he had bought near Bergen and by 2003 ROBBE was inside. Since then her old cockpit and doghouse have been removed and the plan is to restore her to her original layout. And so ROBBE is currently taking time out, as most Windfalls do for periods, but no doubt in due course she will return.

SEA SCAMP

Ex ZEISIG, SEA SCAMP (see a 1951 photograph of her in Chapter 4) is a 50 sq m Windfall built by Abeking and Rasmussen for the Luftwaffe in 1936, has a long pedigree and is still at sea today. She is of particular interest because she is still sailing and also of recent correspondence between her present owners and an ex German Naval officer Herr Meyer who sailed her in the 1941-43 period.

Zeisig (later Sea Scamp) with German crew in 1943

SEA SCAMP was sailed to England in 1946 via the Dutch canals by a lively naval crew with Morin Scott as skipper, his second Windfall delivery, the first being SEETAUBE (See Chapter 4). She was allocated to the Royal Marines training group based at their barracks at Plymouth and remained there until being transferred in 1956 to HMS FISGARD, an apprentices training establishment just across the Tamar in Cornwall. Ten years later she was allocated to nearby HMS RALEIGH, a training establishment for new recruits where she was remain until 1974 to see out her Royal Naval service. Thus SEA SCAMP was always very firmly a West Country yacht throughout her Royal Naval service.

It was not until 1984 that John Kapp happened to hear from Tony Venables at an Offshore Cruising Club party that SEA SCAMP had appeared in the Admiralty Small Craft Disposal List. To quote John "*Without thinking, I said at once 'let's buy her'. Nobody had set eyes on her, let alone surveyed her. The bid had to be delivered to the Admiralty's office in Bath by noon on the following Monday, in 36 hours time. Then Philip Benbridge walked by. Tony said 'Philip, you can deliver a letter to Bath for us can't you'? 'Yes' he said. We then and there got a piece of paper and wrote an offer of about £9,000, which we did not have. Why did we take such an impulsive and irrational decision? The conventional project approach would have been to assess the demand cost the supply options, raise the money and find the boat. This would have taken years, and no boat would ever have been bought that way because we would never have agreed."*

This then is exactly in character with wooden boat acquisition: there is often an element of judgement from the heart rather than via a clinical business assessment. So often when discussing Windfalls one hears similar stories. How many of us have bought houses or boats on impulse, with no survey but with a gut feel that is never regretted.

And so SEA SCAMP came into civilian hands with a refreshing flourish. A syndicate was formed and she joined MARABU which John had bought earlier in 1978. He was running RYA courses and wanted a smaller yacht with similar handling characteristics, so SEA SCAMP fitted the bill well. She was to give good service for these courses over the ensuing years until later, in the 1990s a separate SEA SCAMP syndicate took over the running and to this day she is in constant use, based at Southampton. Her programme in recent years has followed a regular pattern: into the water at Easter followed by week-end and local cruising for a month. Then three months or so Summer cruising, mostly to the West Country, Channel Islands and Brittany. From time to times she has spread her wings further, to Holland, the West coast of Scotland, Ireland and down as far

Sea Scamp in 2007
Martin Hayden

as the Gironde. At present there are hopes for a Baltic trip but long deliveries are hard to find crews for. At 70 years of age she has shown that by the quality of her construction supported by dedicated upkeep of her owners she has many years to go yet.

It was in early 2004 that a Wilhelm Meyer from Hamburg wrote a speculative letter to the Elephant Boatyard on the Hamble, asking if they had any knowledge of the whereabouts of both OVERLORD and SEA SCAMP. He had sailed both yachts (then PELIKAN and ZEISIG) before and during the 2nd World War and indeed had met his future wife sailing them. The boatyard duly passed the letter on to the Offshore Cruising Club who quickly made contact with Herr Meyer and in due course he wrote an article for the SEA SCAMP Journal. It is reproduced at Appendix 10 with the kind permission of the SEA SCAMP Syndicate and of course Herr-Meyer's family (he having since died). Here is yet another example of goodwill generated by the Windfalls, in this case between individuals from nations who had formerly been adversaries.

PINTA (ex BRUNHILDE)

BRUNHILDE, a 50 sq m Windfall, was sailed to England from Kiel in July 1946 by a Naval crew and in due course allocated to the Royal Artillery Yacht Club (RAYC). She later became BRYNHILD then BRYNMERE, based as the club yacht at Cracknore Hard, Southampton. In that year the RAYC, under the auspices of the Association of Services Yacht Clubs (ASYC) won the coveted Royal Yacht Squadron Gold Cup at Seaview against all-comers from the three services. In 1948 the club had a new yacht built and BRYNMERE was moved up to the Clyde. Later in 1952 she was sailed back to Germany for use by the Royal Artillery Yacht Club of the British Army on the Rhine (BAOR). She was put to very good use there and in 1956 was one of the BAOR team of three yachts in the Royal Ocean Racing Club race from Kiel to Marstrand in Sweden. The other two yachts were the 100 sq m KRANICH and the 50 sq m SEA FALCON, both Windfalls. By 1968 BRYNMERE was becoming uneconomical and she was sold in 1970, supposedly to the son of the man who had ordered her from Abeking and Rasmussen before the war, the yacht order being overtaken by the Kriegsmarine. He sailed her until 1985 then sold her to another German in 1986.

Her life was completely changed in 1988 when she was bought by Fred and Heather Bouter from Holland. Her restoration became a labour of love over a number of years in the yard of Benno Rexwinkle and she has now emerged as perhaps the best of the 50 sq m Windfalls at sea today. Fred's account below of that time gives a flavour of how owners become ingrained with the history of their charge, a feature very common in owners of classic boats everywhere.

I am lying on my back in the forepeak feet facing aft. I have been stretching and reaching to put the final layer of Rapid Clear on the new set of sweat planks. Tin of varnish just clear of my ankles paint brush in hand. I only just fit into the space that from now on will again be the storing space for lines, fenders and possibly the grandchildren when they cannot make it back home in time for a sound sleep in their own bed after a good day's sailing. They would fit in there, all three of them together, for another year or so, after which they will outgrow the space. They will not run the risk of being strangled in their bunks by an unruly anchor chain as PINTA has now been equipped with a proper chain locker during the complete renovation. It has shortened her forepeak cabin a bit but with a manhole and inspection hatch we can still inspect the internal hull to the very top of the stem timbers. Between my feet I can see the forward cabin which is still original, as it is shown on the drawings and constructed in 1937 at the Abeking und Rasmussen yard. Efforts to equip the forward cabin with a bit of luxury have failed. No intimate love nest for two. The mast between the two berths was prohibitive. Benno's measuring efforts were to no avail. Looking into the main cabin I notice that Benno has replaced all the old bulkheads: they had become brittle with age and now have been replaced perfectly. We had agreed to stick to Abeking und Rasmussen's drawings but adapted to include a full bulkhead at the rear cockpit wall.

PINTA has come a long way from 'BRUNHILDE' to 'BRYNHILD' to 'BRYNMERE' to 'PINTA II' to 'PINTA', successively flying the German, British and Dutch civil and military flags while serving German and British military and civil owners. She has been stationed in Germany, in the UK and back to Germany and finally to Holland Over seventy years from regatta yacht to training yacht and then to pleasure craft through peace and war, through praise and

50 sq m Brynhild (now Pinta) in 1947
Beken of Cowes

doom, under capable and sometimes less capable skippers, she has been caressed and cursed by flag officers and ordinary seamen alike. To them she has provided both training, recreation and the hospitality of a bunk.

Lying there I felt a faint murmur of fear and fun, why had they all come and where had they all gone. I know where Skipper Don Martin went, but not what happened to KzS Fricke, her skipper in the Kieler Woche (Kiel Week) of 1937. Don skippered her while she was serving time with the British Kiel Yacht Club following a strict training regime. From Monday morning 08.00 hours until Friday afternoon 17.00 hours or earlier in the event that 500 nautical miles had passed between bow and rudder, routinely producing brothers in arms for a week or so but friends for life. Club and training yachts have more experience than family cruisers. Not a place for grandchildren in those days.

The relatively cheap fleet of square metre yachts trained thousands of crews that unfortunately later had to face up to war situations, life or death for you or your mate. Operational losses, also during training, were accepted. Nowadays managers *pay heavily for courses that mould them into teams, Boardroom Teams. PINTA always seems to get what she wants, and she did not want what was being planned for her, to become a Windfall and then just fade away.*

Our family had been sailing along quite happily in their 24 feet Samurai, plenty of crawling room and not difficult or expensive to maintain. Sometimes a bit rough at sea but otherwise ok. On a sunny Saturday afternoon in came PINTA. She appeared through the telephone via word of mouth from a friend who shared ownership in the Samurai. Size, standing room, mahogany, oak and brass and the promise of less seasickness worked miracles on Mrs Bouter and an inspection trip was soon planned to the marina of Wendtorf near Kiel, Germany. It was love at first sight.

Pinta re-emerging as a new condition 50 sq m Windfall. 2007
Rowan Bouter

And so PINTA has been superbly restored and will attend the Kiel Regatta in the summer of 2007, seventy years after her construction and in as perfect condition.

GRIFFIN, later KESTREL, (ex SEEJUNGFER)

There is a little gentle mystery about her birth, as if she was not quite legitimate. Her registration plate is missing but there is little doubt that she was built by Abeking & Rasmussen, not as the 50 sq m SEEJUNGFER as always understood but as SEENIXE, build number 3174. Subsequently she was listed as SEEJUNGFER and is referred to as such in British Admiralty correspondence after the war before being named GRIFFIN, as we have seen an unfortunate choice in that the Royal Ocean Racing Club's yacht was also GRIFFIN. Owned by the Royal Naval College Dartmouth, after three seasons' minor confusion in RORC races her name was sensibly changed to GRYPHIS.

Along with the five other college Windfalls, GRYPHIS had the luxury of being fully maintained at government expense, being used for official seamanship training by the naval cadets. Accordingly she enjoyed 14 years of good racing and cruising with sound sails and annual refits under the college banner. Transferred to the Naval Air Command in 1959 and now under her new name KESTREL, from then on she was sailed from the Portsmouth area then naval outstations in a mainly cruising and adventure training role. Her last naval station was at the Royal Naval Air Station Culdrose, Cornwall, where the author looked after her for a period, by that time rightly not properly funded as focus was put on a brand new Naval Air Command yacht. And so in 1967 she sailed away from 30 years service with the German and Royal Navies to start a new life.

First to pick up the baton was Ted Steele, who ran a motorbike business in London. He put a BMC diesel engine into her and with others sailed "with

50 sq m Kestrel leaving the Helford, 1967
Author on helm

rotten canvas sails" out of Shoreham. The next owner was a lorry driver from Manchester before (falling off the back of a lorry?) she was bought by a C H Bell of Deganwy Yacht Services. Ownership then passed to Joe Mitchell, where at that stage she was stripped out and substantially rebuilt, keeping the same engine. And so it was that she was in a relatively good state when acquired by John Kapp in January 1990 as part of the MARABU syndicate. From then on, under properly funded syndicate ownership, she was once more on the way up, well utilised for RYA courses and syndicate cruises, based at Brighton Marina. Because of the time factor when running courses she was sailed principally in the Channel and round to south Brittany, very successfully. Eventually the syndicate reluctantly decided to dispose of her and in 2004 she was sold to Christopher Dean. She is now lying in Ipswich.

50 sq m Kestrel with RYA Training Course 1990 (N. C. Hall)

CHAPTER 13. So where are they today?

This will necessarily be the most incomplete chapter in the book. It can never be complete but here at least is a start, in alphabetical order, to record where Windfalls are known to be now (2007). It is common for yacht names to be changed, further complicating the picture so for simplicity the first English name has been used. No doubt there are many still out there, or if they are not their demise may be known.

AVALANCHE (ex STORCH) 100 sq m. She was at the British Kiel Yacht Club until 2001, was then bought by Dirk Wilson who intends to use her for classic boat charter, based at Lubecke, near Kiel.

AVALON (ex ALLEMANNE) 30 sq m. After WW 2 she first went to the British Kiel Yacht Club, then, "still in the hands of the British", she sank outside Faaborg (Denmark) during a regatta in the late 1950's. After two or three Danish owners she came back to Germany under the ownership of Rudiger Schach in Hamburg, who restored her to near perfect condition and has sailed her extensively including to Sweden.

BRUNHILDE 50 sq m. Also **BRYNMERE** now **PINTA.** After many adventures she was bought by Fred and Heather Bouter, who brought her to Holland where she has undergone a complete rebuild. She is about to emerge as one of the very best 50 sq m Windfalls at sea today. See Chapter 12. Notable Windfalls.

DISDAINE (ex SEETAUBE) 50 sq m. Is based at Weymouth and is laid up each winter at Portland, Dorset. She was bought from the Admiralty in 1965 by Phil Hutchings and Dave Bishop, who have owned her ever since.

50 sq m Disdaine (ex Seetaube) 2007

DUHNEN 85 ft Schooner. Having reached Calshot in 1945 she was sold in 1946 to an American couple, the author, adventurer and sail training pioneer Irving Johnson and his wife Electa. They had her refitted as a Brigantine by JW & A Upham shipyard at

Brixham, renamed her YANKEE and sailed round the world via the Galapagos Islands, the South Pacific and South East Asia. Later they replaced her with a second YANKEE and in other hands the DUHNEN was stranded in the Cook Islands on 23 July 1964 and subsequently broke up. And so ended the life of the largest of the Windfall fleet.

FLAMINGO 100 sq m. She is still (2007) at the British Kiel Yacht Club, used for cruising and adventure training and is the last Windfall in service with the British forces.

GALAHAD (ex ADLER) (90 sq m) For years the principal Windfall of the Royal Naval Engineering College at Plymouth, she was replaced in 1959 and disappeared. Years later Peter Archer thought that he saw her without a mast, then a houseboat on the Thames.

100 sq m Flamingo. Winter refit at Kiel 2006

GLADEYE Also **EISVOGEL (ex REIHER)** 100 sq m. She is currently lying in Southern Portugal and is in some need of refurbishment.

GRIFFIN (ex SEEJUNGFER) later **GRYPHIS** then **KESTREL** 50 sq m. Another of the ex Dartmouth yachts, she is now lying at Ipswich.

KESTREL See GRIFFIN

100 sq m Gladeye (ex Reiher) in Portugal 2007

HAWK 50 sq m. As we have seen in Chapter 7, her bones have laid at the bottom of the English Channel since August 1957, together with Midshipman Ryan's dinner jacket and fruit cake.

KRANICH 100 sq m. After her long service in the Baltic she was finally disposed of by the services in about 1995 and was last heard of in 1999 at Kaltonhof, Germany.

LEOPARD (ex NORBEC) Now **TARMAIN** 50 sq m. Last heard of at Sandpoint Marine Services, Dunbarton.

LIVELY (ex A.R.) 125 sq m. Now in Hamburg, Germany.

MARABU 100 sq m. See Chapter 12. Notable Windfalls. She is now laid up in Ipswich.

MERLIN (ex WAL) 100 sq m. Her history is recalled in Chapter 12. Now called ZEEAREND, she is fully restored and a credit to the owner, Leo Aarens and based in Holland.

NORDWIND 60 ton yawl. It is appropriate that the Windfall which was the pride of the German Kriegsmarine fleet before the war should still be at sea today in pristine condition following a total rebuild completed in 2003. NORDWIND is currently to be seen in the Mediterranean and the West Indies, a tribute to her builders and the loving care of many owners. See Chapter 12. Notable Windfalls.

ORION In her naval service she was based on the Clyde and was the only Windfall to complete the Fastnet Race in 1947, the first race after the war. At 78 ft length over all and 31 tons she was a powerful figure in the Scottish racing scene, including Clyde Weeks. Her bones are reported to have been seen in Fareham Creek but with her draft that may be unlikely.

OSTERLING 30 sq m. Last heard of in Cheshire.

OVERLORD (ex PELIKAN) See Chapter 12. Notable Windfalls. She is now the last 100 sq m Windfall in UK waters. She is operated by a syndicate under the banner of the Offshore Cruising Club and has a very extensive cruising programme each year. When not at sea she is berthed in the Solent.

PEGASUS Now **HILTGUND** Was also **SEA VICTOR** 50 sq m. She has had a very varied career. Having been one of the fully public funded 50 sq m yachts at the Royal Naval College from 1946 to 1959, she was transferred to the Royal Naval barracks at Portsmouth under the new name of SEA VICTOR where she cruised

100 sq m Overlord (ex Pelikan) 2007

and raced from the Solent area. There she remained until 1965 until she was disposed of by the Navy and returned to her old German name HILTGUND. After changing hands several times she was acquired in 1990 by Malcolm Brown but she was in a very bad way with a damaged hull and did not go forwards. And so it was that in 1996 she was bought by Peter Wilson and totally refitted by the Aldeburgh Boatyard Company, who did a superb job. For a period she had a successful racing career on the East Coast and in 1998 was third overall in the Hermes Mumm Regatta. It was in 2001 that she was transferred to Scottish waters and since then has been cruised and raced by John and Jilly Bourke and Chris Perring on the West Coast.

PHOENIX (ex BUKANIER) 30 sq m. Has been completely refurbished by Paul and Lorraine Holmes and sails out of Saltash, Plymouth.

PICKLE (ex HELGOLAND) 30 ton yawl. Although first reported as being abandoned as a hulk she was in fact completely rebuilt and is now (2007) up for sale at Gaspe, Peninsula, Quebec. She has now resumed her original name HELGOLAND. See Chapter 11, Windfalls Abroad.

PINTA See BRUNHILDE

RASMUS 42 ft Ketch. With FLAMINGO and KRANICH she was the third long term Windfall at the British Kiel Yacht Club, finally being sold in 1992. She is still seaworthy and is now laid up (winter 2006/2007) just a few yards away from her old home in an adjacent yard at Stickenhorn.

ROBBE 100 sq m. She is now (2007) in a boat shed in Bergen, Norway. Her cruising logs for the 1950 to 1958 period are held at the library in the Royal Military Academy Sandhurst.

ROSANNA 50 sq m. She was disposed of in the Mediterranean in 1956 and has not been heard of since.

100 sq m Robbe in Norway with large doghouse

SEA EAGLE (ex SEEFALKE II) (also Sea Falcon) 50 sq m. After the war she was retained briefly at Kiel under the Royal Artillery Yacht Club burgee before being transferred to Southampton for the RAYC Larkhill group in 1947. She went back to Kiel in 1954 and was sold there in 1960. It is understood that she has been completely refurbished.

SEA SCAMP (ex ZEISIG) 50 sq m. She is still in service with the SEA SCAMP Syndicate, based in the Solent and looking very trim, still with her wooden mast. See Chapter 12. Notable Windfalls.

SEA SOLDIER (ex SEEFALKE I) 50 sq m. After her service career with the Royal Marines she was put on the Disposals list in 1968. At some stage she was apparently "acquired by two doctors" before her present owner Lynn Roach bought her in 1988, who refitted her in Glamorgan over a period. Now renamed SEEFAULKE. She then made history when she was sailed by her owner to Antigua in 1996, the first and only 50 sq m Windfall known to have crossed the Atlantic. In 1998 she added further to her stature when she became the overall winner of the Antigua Classic Regatta. She then sailed on to America, losing her wooden mast on the way and continuing to New York under jury rig. She has no engine. In due course she returned to Antigua and now lies in English Harbour where she is up for sale should a suitable buyer appear.

SEA FEATHER (ex SEEFEDER) 50 sq m. Last seen in Anglesy in the 1990's.

SEA HEXE (ex SEEHEXE) 50 sq m. Bought from the Belsize boatyard in Southampton in 1972, she sailed the Bristol Channel for 22 years before starting a refurbishment programme. Last seen at Newport, Gwent in 1996.

SEA LION (ex AUSTERNFISCHER) 100 sq m. She was lost off Alderney in 1955 or 1956 but curiously no account of this has yet been found in French or Channel Island press records. From several reliable sources it was established that she apparently lost her mast in bad weather and accepted a tow. As so often happens when a larger ship tows a yacht there are problems and apparently she broke up or was driven under. Certainly from then on she disappeared from the Lloyds Yacht Register and the RAF replaced her with a new yacht LADY CORINNE. The photograph shown here is of a painting of SEA LION by R. Pearson with Professor Jimmy Macworth's father at the helm.

SEEOTTER 50 sq m. After an illustrious career in the ownership of the late Peter Richardson, she is now lying at Porchester, Hants.

30 sq m Suna ashore in Hove

SPERLING 50 sq m. Last heard of at Sheffield.

SUNA 30 sq m. She was bought privately by John Kapp in 1996 with the intention of including her in his MARABU/ KESTREL Syndicate but this was in fact not done and she remained a separate venture. Partially refurbished in John's garden in Hove, she was transferred to Portsmouth and the work completed over the following two years. A SUNA Syndicate was formed with a group from the north and John still remains part of it. The yacht now sails out of Liverpool and the syndicate would appreciate more members.

SUNSTREAM 30 sq m. Having been sailed by the Highland Brigade Yacht Club in her time in the services she was put on the Admiralty Disposal List and sold in September 1956. After a succession of seven owners, mainly in the Solent area, she is currently lying near Falmouth, Cornwall where she is undergoing an extensive rebuild.

30 sq m Sunstream 2007

TANGAIKA (ex LEUCHTAFER) 50 sq m. In the early 1990's she was last seen in Auckland, New Zealand.

EPILOGUE

Perhaps the main lesson to come out of this unusual Windfall story is the quite extraordinary amount of good that has come out of it. Little did the German government imagine that their decision in the 1930s to build a fleet of yachts and smaller craft for their services would have such a beneficial effect for many decades to come and indeed to this day. Countless experiences of the sea

German crew 1930s

have been gained, countless friendships made, sometimes for life. They particularly enhanced the lives of those who sailed them during a difficult period after the war. Windfalls found their way into the waters of not only Europe but countries across the world, from New Zealand to Canada. A Windfall yacht won the prodigious Championship of the Mediterranean in 1952 and a Windfall dinghy took part in the 1952 Olympics at Helsinki.

Today there are sponsored crewed races round the globe such as the Volvo Race at hitherto unbelievable speeds. Before that were the Whitbread Races, the early ones in the 1970s organised by the RNSA and included non sponsored services entries. These organisers and sailors were all introduced to sailing in the Windfall yachts. The influence of the Windfalls has thus played its part in overall development of British offshore sailing, far beyond their concept in the 1930s.

Essentially the boats were built in the 1930s for young people to learn about seamanship, navigation and self reliance, an ethic which has been continued to this day seventy years later. Thousands upon thousands of mainly young people have sailed in the Windfalls, many getting their first sailing experiences in them. Many in turn became yacht skippers and experienced that peculiar thrill of realising that "the buck stops with me". All learnt many lessons about sailing and indeed themselves, always gaining from it.

That these wooden yachts were so well built is amply demonstrated by the fact that in all their history only two have been known to have been lost offshore at sea (one, having lost her mast her hull was then damaged alongside a rescue ship and the second having lost her mast was sunk under tow) in an era when several well found wooden racing yachts broke up. Naturally over such a long period they experienced their share of exceptionally heavy weather such as in the notorious 1956 Channel Race when the crack Class 1 yacht BLOODHOUND was abandoned, only five yachts finished out of twenty-three yet the 50 sq m Windfall SEA HEXE won her class. While a number of Windfalls lost their hollow wooden masts in the later years their hulls stood up over many years to storms in European waters and across the Atlantic, including a 50 sq m yacht, a tribute to their design and construction.

So this has been a glimpse of the Windfall yachts, remembered by so many with affection and some still sailed with pride. As with all research there is always more to be uncovered but perhaps that in itself is an attraction. Nothing is forever and in the fullness of time all the Windfalls will have gone. Here then is at least a start to document this unique and somewhat unusual episode in our national maritime history. A legacy of goodwill indeed.

English Crew 1950s

APPENDICES

Appendices:

APPENDIX 1
MASTER LIST OF 100 SQUARE
METRE WINDFALL YACHTS

English Name	German Name	Built	Builder	Sail No	First allocated to
Avalanche	Storch	1936	GKW	XI 7	Royal Engineer Yacht Club
Flamingo	Flamingo	1935	A & R	X9	British Kiel Yacht Club
Gladeye (a)	Reiher	1935	A & R	X8	Household Division.
Konigin	Konigin	1935	A & R	X6	BKYC then to German owner
Kranich	Kranich	1936	GKW	XI 6	British Kiel Yacht Club
Marabu	Marabu	1935	A & R	XI0	HMS Excellent
Overlord	Pelikan	1936	A & R	XI 3	Royal Engineer Yacht Club
Robbe	Robbe	1937	BM	XI 8	Army School of Infantry
Sea Lion	Austernfischer	1936	A & R	XI 2	Royal Air Force Yacht Club
Wal(b)	Wal	1938	BM	XI 9	HMS Collingwood

Notes: (a)   Later Eisvogel
      (b)   Later Collingwood then Wal then Merlin then Zeearend
           GKW: Gerdhardt Kroger Werft
           A & R: Abeking and Rasmussen
           BM: Burmester

APPENDIX 2
MASTER LIST OF 50 SQUARE METRE
WINDFALL YACHTS

English Name	German Name	Built	Builder	Sail No	First Allocated To
Anneliese	Anneliese				BKYC
Ase	Ase				BKYC
Brynhilde	Brunhilde*	1937	A & R	V97	RAYC
Cyclops					See Meon Maid
Disdaine	Seetaube*	1938	A & R	V104	RN Engineering College
Flimm					See Kuckuck
Glilse					Canada
Goldamer	Goldamer**	1936	A & R	V39	RAF YC
Griffin	Seejungfer*	1937	A & R	V26	BRNC. Later Kestrel
Gryphis					See Griffin
Harpy	Gunther	1938	Vertens	V95	BRNC. Not true 50 sq m
Hawk	Seesturm*(a)	1937	A & R	V59	BRNC. Sank 1957
Joste	Joste				BKYC
Kestrel					See Griffin
Kuckuck	Kuckuck	1936	A & R	V44	BKYC. Later Flimm
Leopard	Norbec*	1937		V100	BRNC. Later Tarmain
Lerche	Lerche**	1935	A & R	V36	RAF YC
Martlet	Wotan*	1937	A & R	V54	BRNC
Meise	Meise**	1936	A & R	V42	RAF
Meon Maid	Drossel*	1936	A & R	V31	HMS Mercury
Mosquito	Musquito*	1938	Lloydwft	V63	Not Known
Pegasus	Hiltgund*	1938	M & P	V85	BRNC. Also Sea Victor
Pinta					See Brynhilde
Pirol	Pirol**	1935	A & R	V37	RAF Coastal Command SA
Rosanna	Seemelke*				Malta's only 50 sq m RAYC
Sea Breeze	Seebrise*	1937	A & R	V98	HMS Hawke

MASTER LIST OF 50 SQUARE METRE
WINDFALL YACHTS

English Name	German Name	Built	Builder	Sail No	First Allocated To
Sea Hexe	Seehexe*	1936		V48	Naval Air Command
Sea Eagle	Seefalke II*	1937	A & R		Royal Artillery YC
Sea Feather	Seefeder*	1937		V81	HMS Ganges
Seeforelle	Seeforelle		A & R	V57	BKYC
Sea Horse	Seepferdchen*	1938			RN Barracks Portsmouth
Sea Otter	Seeotter*	1936	A & R	V50	HMS Vernon
Seerauber	Seerauber*	1938	Rathje	V23	
Sea Scamp	Zeisig*	1936	A & R	V43	Royal Marines
Sea Soldier	Seefalke I*	1935	A & R	V30?	Royal Marine Barracks
Sea Swallow	Seeschwalbe*	1935	BM	V81	HMS Defiance
Sea Victor					See Pegasus
Sea Wraith	Seegeist*	1937	Howaid	V48	HMS Excellent
Seeotter					See Sea Otter
Sperling	Sperling**	1936			RAF
Tangaika	Leuchtafer				New Zealand
Tarmain					See Leopard
Theodora	Theodoric				BKYC. RAC YC
Thor	Thor*	1938	M & P	V92	Late shipment to UK
Topsy II	Dompfaff*	1935	A & R	V36	RN Engineering College
Torch	Seemowe*	1936		V41	REYC. Also Seamew
Tuna					Canada

*		Operation HOMEWARD
**		Operation SALLYPORT
Acronyms		See Page 192

Note: (a) Originally SEENIXE.

APPENDIX 3
MASTER LIST OF 30 sq m
WINDFALL YACHTS

English Name	German Name	Built	Builder	First Allocated To
Aase	Aase			Gibraltar
Angela	Gote	1936	A & R	Malta
Aurora	Austerling			Army
Avalon	Allemane	1936	A & R	BKYC
Cito				Royal Signals Sailing Assoc
Erida	Erida			Hamble 1956-65
Falkland	Coronel	1938		RAF
Filibuster	Filibuster			BKYC
Flandern	Flandern			Woolwich then Malta
Freibeuter	Freibeuter			BKYC
Friese	Friese	1936	A & R	BKYC
Germane	Germane			
Gernet	Gernot	1938	A & R	Malta. Hal Far
Geuse	Geuse	1936	A & R	BKYC
Heiko	Heiko	1937	A & R	BKYC
Holste	Holste	1937	A & R	Admiralty 1947 list
Irouswich	Irouswich			Army 1947
Korsar	Korsar			BKYC
Lady Elsa	Lady Elsa			HMS Caledonia
Likedeeler	Likedeeler			BKYC
Max	Max			Malta. Poor condition
Meerkonig	Meerkonig			BKYC
Moritz	Moritz			Airborne Forces
Murwic II	Murwic II			RAF Calshot 1947
Osterling	Osterling			Now in Cheshire
Pelikan	Pelikan			BKYC

MASTER LIST OF 30 sq m
WINDFALL YACHTS

English Name	German Name	Built	Builder	First Allocated To
Phoenix	Bukanier	1936	A & R	Malta
Pirat	Pirat			BKYC
Plum	Ploem			Malta
Saluki	Seejungfer			Army. Malta
Sachse	Sachse			RASCYC
Schwalbe II	Schwalbe II	1937	A & R	Australia
Suna	Aegir	1936	A & R	Gibraltar then Malta
Sunstream	Sunstream	1939	Vertens	Highland Brigade Yacht Club
Trove	Trove			Lossiemouth
Vandale	Vandale			BKYC
Vitalienbruder	Vitalienbruder	1935	A & R	BKYC

Acronyms   See Page 192

APPENDIX 4
MASTER LIST OF MISCELLANEOUS WINDFALL YACHTS

English Name	German Name	Type	Built	First Allocated to
Aegir X	Aegir X	150 sq m		BKYC
Asta	Asta	57 ton yawl	1894	Unallocated Feb 1947
Capella	Borkum	90 sq m	1938	RNVR
Corsair	Korsar	40 ft cutter	1938	HMS St Vincent 1955
Duhnen	Duhnen	85 ft Schooner	1912	Sold on arrival in UK
Edith VII	Edith VII	35 tons		Unallocated late 1946
Galahad	Adler	85 sq m	1921	RNEC. Later Aquilla
Godecke Michel	Godecke Michel	189 sq m		Ketch. Unallocated late 1946
Heimat	Heimat	52 ft ketch	1924	Sold on arrival in UK
Husky	Seewolf	26 ton ketch		REYC
Jacunda	Jacunda	150 sq m		BKYC
Joass	Joass	39 sq m		RN Nore Branch
Jutta	Jutta	39 sq m	1938	RN Nore Branch
Kormoran	Cormoran	50 ft ketch	1929	RAF
Lady Eve	Lady Eve	90 sq m		Disposed of 1946
Lively	Lively	125 sq m		BKYC
Melba	Melba	90 sq m?		Disposed of 1946
Nimrod	Neck	39 sq m		RN. Portland
Nordwind	Nordwind	60 ton yawl	1939	Sold on arrival in UK
Orion	Orion	150 sq m	1910	RN. Clyde
Paul Benecke	Paul Benecke	28 ton yawl	1921	Unallocated late 1946
Pickle	Helgoland	30 ton yawl	1938	Canada. Also described cutter
Planet	Planet	60 sq m	1910	HMS Dryad
Rasmus	Rasmus	42 ft ketch	1928	BKYC

MASTER LIST OF MISCELLANEOUS WINDFALL YACHTS

English Name	German Name	Type	Built	First Allocated to
Seagram	Nordost	60 sq m		Later Silver Tassie
Seeadler	Seeadler	45 sq m		BKYC
Seedrache	Seedrache	60 ft yawl	1937	ex Luftwaffe
Seerquer	Seerquer	60 ft ketch	1911	ex Luftwaffe
Seestern	Seestern	40 ft ketch	1923	ex Luftwaffe
Sigrid	Sigrid	22 tons		Clyde. To be sold 1955
Skagerrak	Skagerrak	60 ton yawl	1938	
Victoria		80 sq m		Kiel
Walkure	Walkure	61 ft yaw1	1939	
Wunsch	Wunsch	35 sq m		Sailed to UK early 1947

Acronyms

See Page 192

APPENDIX 5
WINDFALL YACHTS HELD
BY THE RAF IN GERMANY IN 1945
(Mainly ex Luftwaffe Owned)

English Name	German Name	Type	Built	Allocated in UK to
Sea Lion*	Austernfischer	100 sq m	1936	RAF
Avalanche*	Storch	100 sq m	1936	Royal Engineer YC
Gladeye*	Reiher	100 sq m	1935	Household Division
Overlord*	Pelikan	100 sq m	1935	Royal Engineer YC
Kranich**	Kranich	100 sq m	1936	British Kiel Yacht Club
Lerche*	Lerche	50 sq m	1936	RAF
Pirol*	Pirol	50 sq m	1934	RAF
Goldamer*	Goldamer	50 sq m	1935	RAF
Sperling*	Spirlind	50 sq m	1934	RAF
Meise*	Meise	50 sq m	1938	RAF
Husky*	Seewolf	42' Ketch	1937	Royal Engineer YC
Kormoran*	Cormoran	50' Ketch	1929	RAF
Seestern*	Seestern	40' Aux Ketch	1923	Understood disposed of
Duhnen*	Duhnen	85' Schooner	1912	Sold on arrival in UK
	Seequer	60' Ketch	1911	Understood disposed of
	Skedrache	60' Ax Yawl	1937	Understood disposed of
	Heimat*	52' Aux Ketch	1924	Understood disposed of

Sailed or towed to UK with RAF crews
** Remained in Germany

APPENDIX 6 (1)– PLANS OF 100 SQ M WINDFALL

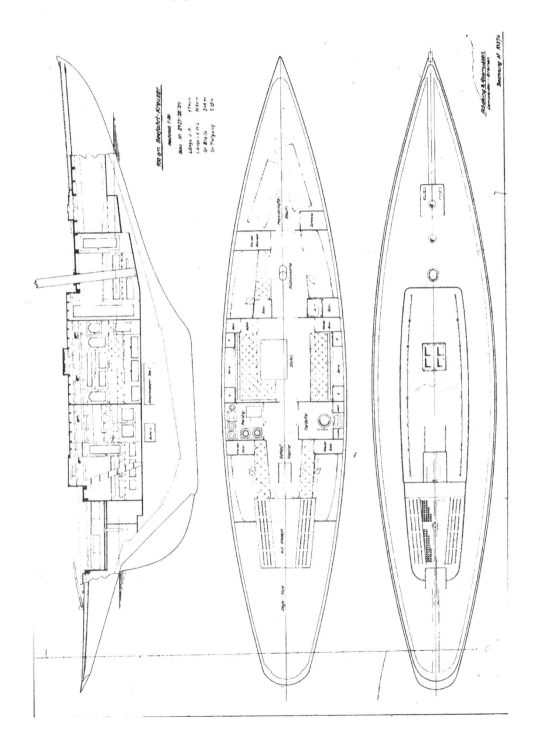

APPENDIX 6 (2) – CROSS SECTION
OF 100 SQ M WINDFALL

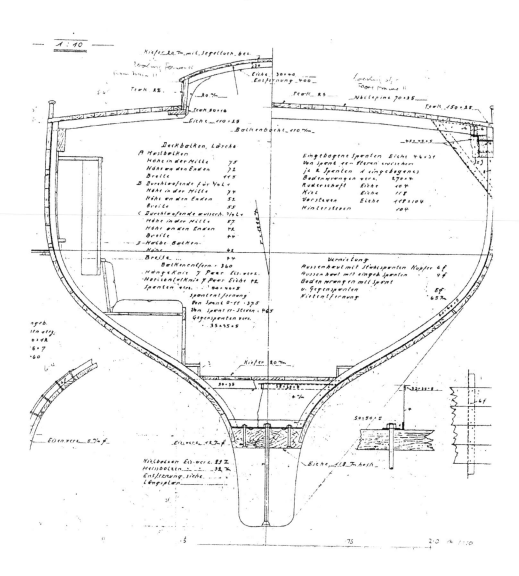

APPENDIX 6 (3) – RIG AND SAILPLAN OF 100 SQ M WINDFALL

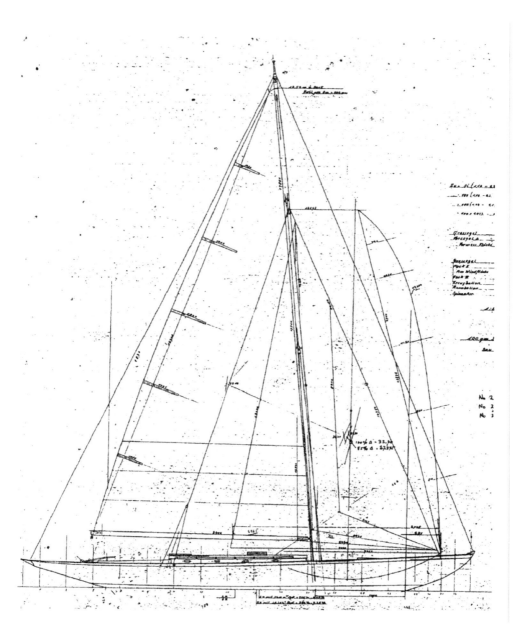

Note. The poor quality of this sailplan is regretted but at the time of going to print no better copies were available. Something is better than nothing.

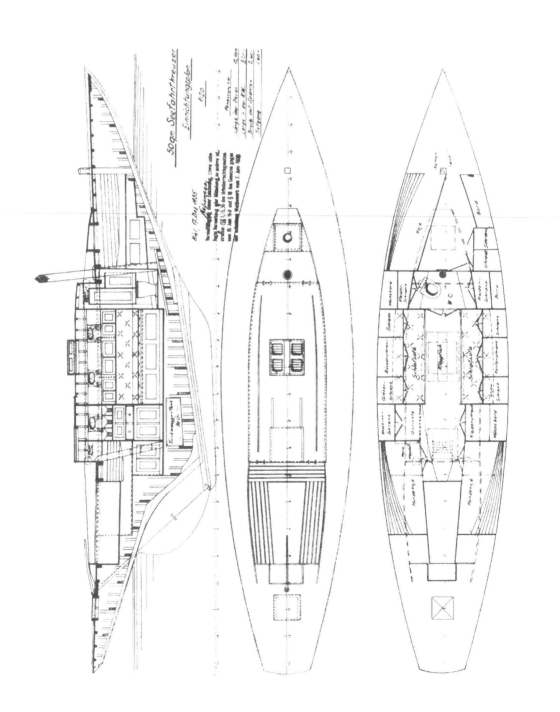

APPENDIX 7 (2) – RIG AND SAILPLAN
OF 50 SQ M WINDFALL

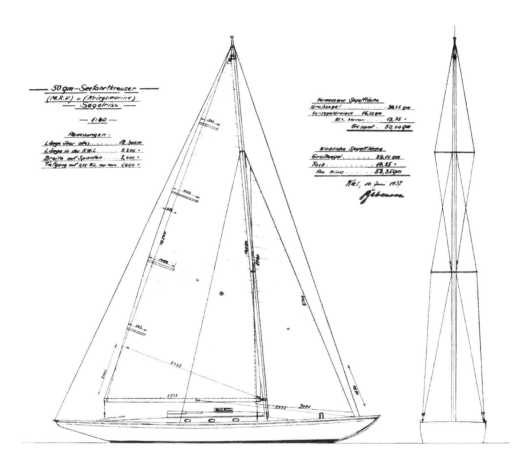

APPENDIX 7 (3) – CROSS SECTION
OF 50 SQ M WINDFALL

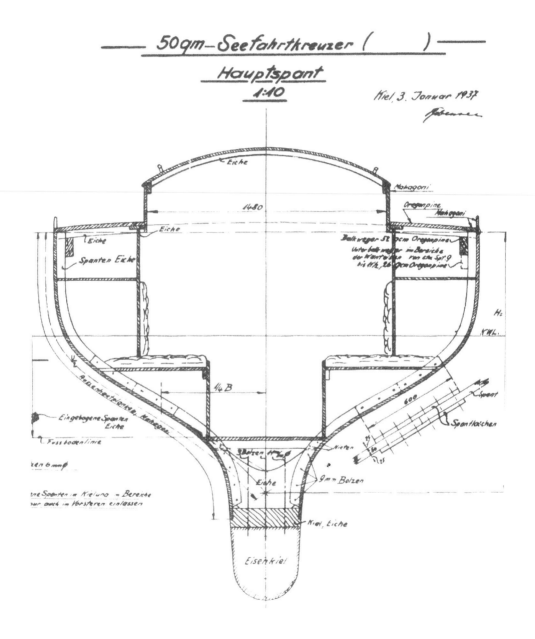

APPENDIX 8 (1) – PLANS OF 30 SQ M WINDFALL

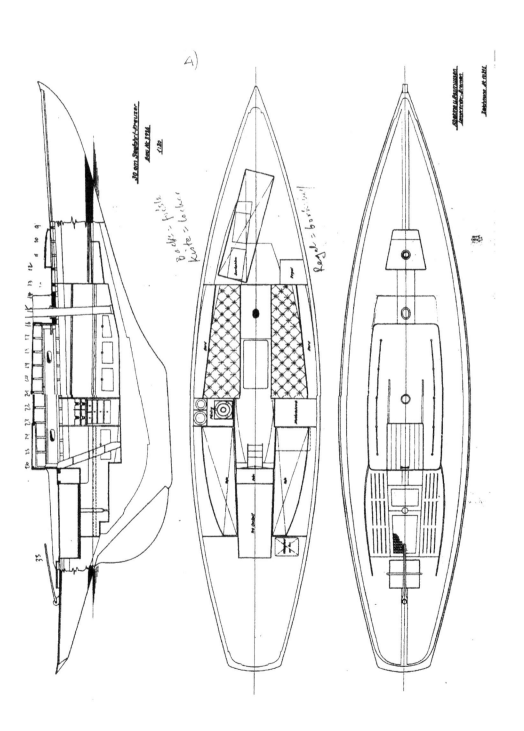

APPENDIX 8 (2) – CROSS SECTION
OF 30 SQ M WINDFALL

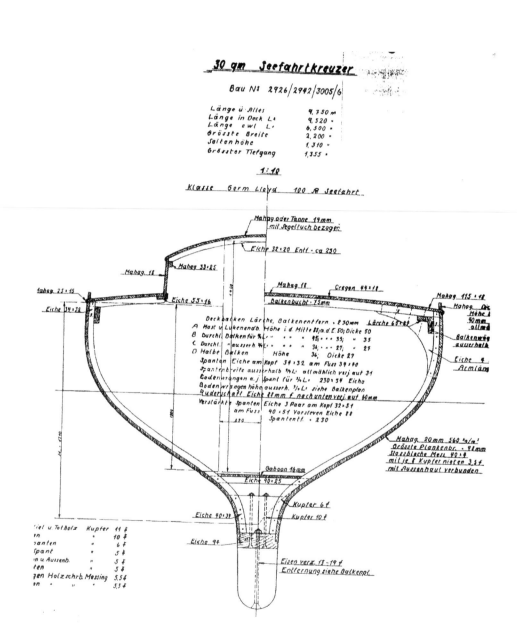

APPENDIX 8 (3) – SAILPLAN OF 30 SQ M WINDFALL

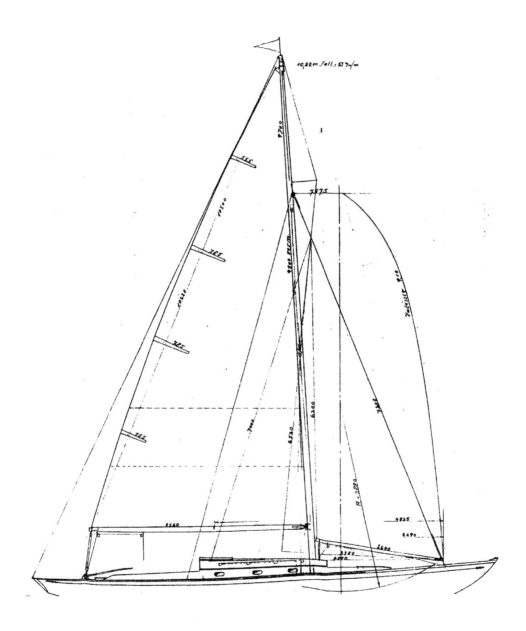

APPENDIX 8 (4) – CONSTRUCTION
OF 30 SQ M WINDFALL

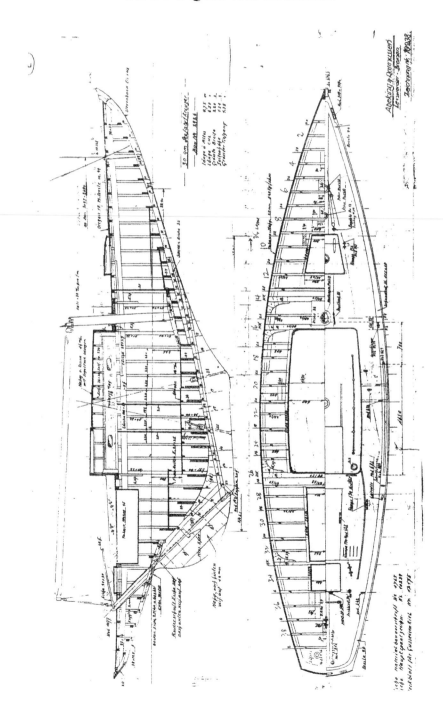

APPENDIX 9. *OPERATION HOMEWARD – Volunteers to sail Naval Windfalls to UK*

The sailing of the naval Windfalls to UK was put under the command of Commander in Chief Portsmouth, who issued a series of orders to the fleet, the first two of which are reproduced below.

PORTSMOUTH GENERAL ORDER 7982. 8 May 1946. Sailing of Ex-German Yachts from Cuxhaven to Portsmouth.

1. *Volunteers are required from serving Naval personnel to sail ex-German yachts from Cuxhaven to Portsmouth.*
2. *There are about 50 of these yachts, ranging from 7 to 60 tons, of which 11 will be fitted out and ready to sail on 12th May. It is anticipated that the remainder will become ready in groups at fortnightly intervals.*
3. *For the 11 yachts ready on 12th May, 10 skippers (one is already in Germany) and 61 hands are needed. It is intended to transport these crews to Cuxhaven by Destroyer sailing about 9th May.*
4. *Names of volunteers to man the first group, stating experience if any, and period for which available, are to be forwarded to my office as early as practicable, and those for subsequent groups as convenient.*
5. *It is anticipated that crews will consist chiefly of officers but ratings who are of a suitable type and who have experience may be included. Crews will vary from about 8 to 4 depending on the size of the yachts. At least 2 members of each crew should have had experience of this type of work. If ships and establishments find it possible to form complete crews, arrangements will be made to sail them together if practicable. Personnel will be considered to be on duty during this operation.*
6. *Information concerning passages, clothing, money, etc will be communicated to volunteers in due course.*

PORTSMOUTH GENERAL ORDER 8041. *Transfer of Ex-German Yachts*
1. *With reference to P.G.O. 7982, the first group of yachts will not now be fitted out and ready to sail until 15th May 1946 and are to be taken over at Kiel, not Cuxhaven.*
2. *A list of the volunteers selected to man this 1st group is shown in the Appendix to this P.G.O. They are to report at the Office of the Commodore, R.N. Barracks, at 1600 on 12th May for final instructions, issue of bedding, etc. H.M.S. SAVAGE will sail with these volunteers at 2000 on 12th May.*
3. *ACCOMMODATION. Accommodation in H.M.S. SAVAGE will be makeshift and crews must be prepared to live hard. Accommodation in*

Germany is also likely to be rough rather than luxurious. Victualling and accommodation is at Admiralty expense and will be arranged by the Naval authorities at the ports visited.

4. MEDICAL. Orders concerning inoculation against typhus are being strictly enforced in Germany. All volunteers who have not had an anti- typhus inoculation within the last six months are to have the first of the series forthwith. The second will be given on passage in the destroyer and the third in Germany.

5. DRESS. Uniform will be the normal rig on passage to Germany and ashore. Volunteers are advised to take one uniform suit with accessories, oilskins, an inflatable lifebelt and a practical sailing rig.

6. BEDDING. Officers will be issued with a hammock and bedding at R.N. Barracks before embarking. Ratings are to bring their own.

7. IDENTIFICATION. Identity cards or pay books are to be carried.

8. MONEY. Sterling will be changed by Naval authorities in Germany, if required. No person is allowed to take more than £10 out of U.K.

9. TRAVELLING EXPENSES. The refund of reasonable travelling expenses has been authorised. Claims submitted on Forms S.542 will be considered on return to Portsmouth.

10. SUBSEQUENT SAILINGS. More volunteers are required to man subsequent groups of yachts. It is anticipated that the next two groups will be ready to sail about 1st June and 15th June.

APPENDIX 10
A German Naval Officer's Memories

In 2004 an ex German Naval Officer, Wilhelm Meyer, made contact with the Offshore Cruising Club and the SEA SCAMP Syndicate. In the war years he had sailed ZEISIG (later SEA SCAMP) and PELIKAN (later OVERLORD) and had always wanted to know what happened to them. He met his wife aboard SEA SCAMP over 60 years ago. To his joy he found that both yachts were (and still are) sailing today and so correspondence developed, yet another example of the goodwill that the Windfalls have generated.

Wilhelm was asked if he would produce an article for the SEA SCAMP journal, which he did. He died recently and his article is reproduced here in abbreviated form with grateful thanks to the SEA SCAMP syndicate.

A Wish Fulfilled!!

I became a soldier on the 9th November 1938 when I was enlisted in the "Air Reconnaissance Troop" at Braunschweig. After my basic training I was transferred to the flying boat squadron in Norderney, where I was able to experience the last summer of peace with wonderful weather and the many people who were spending their holidays there. Because my stay in Norderney was my first contact with the open sea, this time meant a great deal to me because it was here that my love for the sea and its many different boats began.

From Norderney, I was sent to the Military College in Halle where they trained me to become an officer. Subsequently I was transferred to Hornum on the island of Sylt from where the invasion of Norway began. We landed there at the flying boat military airfield Stavanger-Sola-See from where we were engaged in the surveillance of the sea sector towards the Scottish coast. On the 1st January 1941, I was promoted to lieutenant, and after a further short period of service I was redeployed back in Germany to the Air Reconnaissance Sea School as an education officer. (This school was in West-Dievenow on Wollin with its wonderful sailing area!)

Because we had to have sailing instruction for sea reconnaissance work, I immersed myself in this, for me, a completely new field, with great enthusiasm and learnt and understood things quickly. As well as my training course, which I also completed with full participation, I took every available opportunity at the yacht harbour to get to know the boats there better and in order to sail out into the free waters of the Baltic. I was able to sail boats like the Sharpy, jollenkreuzer, ZEISIG (SEA SCAMP) and PELIKAN (OVERLORD). I was therefore able, together with other sailing friends, to dissipate my useful energy in the pursuit of sailing and gathering experience. A major racing regatta for hundred square metre keel boats was organised, and quite naturally our squad was needed and had to participate! As my name was already fairly well known because of a number of successes in previous minor regattas, my commanding officer appointed me as "Helmsman". This regatta stretched over two days. The start was off Greifswald in the Greifswalder Bodden, the finish was also back off Greifswald, but there was an intermediate stop at Labbe on the island of Rügen. To my own great satisfaction and to the great acclamation of all my fellow sailing participants, I won! (Winning Boat PELIKAN.)

Occasionally, opportunities arose at weekends to undertake small private cruises on the Stettiner Haff, Wollen, and Sweinemünde. On one of these cruises with ZEISIG on which my commanding officer had "ordered" me to join him I met a pretty young girl whom I had never seen before as well as my commanding officer, his wife and child. Now, have a guess what came of this! You have guessed correctly: this young girl became my beloved wife and we have now been married for more than sixty one years, (Diamond Wedding). After I had been promoted to first Lieutenant on 1st January 1943, we married on 18th May 1943, and our beloved daughter Ingeborg was born on 19th March 1944.

But now back to the boats which I had not seen again since November 1944. Because we had no fuel at that time, most of the flying clubs and schools were closed. I was transferred to Wittstock/Dosse to a parachute regiment in order to take over a company there. I spent the end of the war near the Hague, and was badly wounded on 2nd May 1945 (I was buried alive as a result of bombing causing major damage to a lung), and released from an English prisoner of war camp on 11th August 1945.

When one could think peaceful thoughts again the "remember, remember" began. Again and again we asked about the whereabouts of the two boats along the Baltic coast. (Kiel, Lubeck, Travemunde etc.) All efforts were in vain. Then someone at NDR-TV (I had worked about thirty years there!) mentioned the publisher of "Yachts" in Hamburg. I made enquiries immediately and to my great joy found the information. I then immediately contacted you and when I saw the pictures with the new names SEA SCAMP and OVERLORD for the first time my fervent wish was realised, and I readily admit that at that moment tears of joy filled my eyes because of my heartfelt emotions. I am so grateful that these two boats are being well looked after by you and I hope that they will continue to have a long and successful sailing life.

I would like to add that I greatly regret not being able to see the two boats, my favourites, last year when you visited Travemunde and that I was not able to walk their decks again. The next time you are in Germany, you must let us know!

From your German sailing friend,
With very best wishes, Wilhelm Meyer

APPENDIX 11
PASSAGE OF THE 50 SQ M WINDFALL
PIROL TO UK IN JUNE 1946

The following abbreviated account of the passage of the 50 square metre Windfall PIROL to UK in June 1946 by an RAF crew is reproduced by kind permission of the magazine "Motorboat and Yachting". It was written in August of that year by two RAF airmen who clearly knew what they were doing in a yacht and the article reflects an "us and them" attitude not recognisable today.

FROM THE BALTIC TO BLIGHTY Log of the Reich Yacht Pirol by R & W Clark

Having just returned from over 3 years in the Far East, we learned that crews were required to bring over ex-Luftwaffe training craft for the R.A.F. Yacht Club. This seemed a perfect way of spending our last few weeks before demobilisation and we promptly volunteered.

On May 28 we arrived at Calshot, the jumping-off place for the expedition, at about 1 p.m. and organised ourselves a meal and a couple of beds for the night. In the afternoon we were summoned to the C.O.'s conference room for a talk. We could hardly see the speakers for Group Captains, and found that only eight of the 70 or so participating were "other ranks. "At this briefing we were told that 14 boats were to be brought back; we were divided into crews and detailed to fly to Schleswig in a Sunderland to join the 50-sq.-metre yacht "Pirol." Our crew was to be Skipper, a Wing Cmdr Pilot, M.O. and navigator, a Sqdn. Ldr., a Pilot and Naval Liaison Officer, and the pair of us.

May 29. We rose early, had breakfast and packed our kits for the start. A motor launch took us to our kite, and we were able to obtain seats in the forward compartment with our gear stowed in the after one. We passed over the Zuider Zee and quite a bit of flooded coast, then over the sea again until we struck the N.E. coast of Germany. We came upon Schleswig unexpectedly, circled the lake and touched down.

Motor launches driven by Germans took us to the camp harbour, and ashore we took a look around the blocks for somewhere to park down and something to eat. The latest gen on the black market was volunteered, and altogether we had a very good evening, although German beer is very weak. Got back to billet at 11.30 p.m., spent an hour looking for blankets and mutually agreed that we were going to like Schleswig.

May 30. Spent the day getting acquainted with the yacht, bent the sails and got her ready for a trial spin. She was 41 ft overall length and 31 ft. on the waterline, beam 8 ft. 6 ins., draught 5 ft. 6 ins. Designed primarily as a racer, she had exceptionally good accommodation. Forward were the fo'c'sle, anchor chain and sail storage, and two pipe cots. Looking aft, to starboard was the entrance to lavatory and saloon (used normally as a hooch locker), amidships the toilet, and a clothes locker to port. The saloon, with full headroom, was furnished with shelves, locker space, and a portable table (not used). Between the saloon and the s.d. cockpit were the galley, and to starboard the after berth, which carried on under the deck. Right aft was a bosun's locker.

May 31. The morning was spent in getting navigation equipment stowed and checked. A German rigger helped us; he had joined the German Navy in 1933, then transferred to the Luftwaffe. We had hoped for a sail during the afternoon, but the idea was squashed by the powers that be. Went to the Malcolm Club again for the evening, but returned to yacht early so as to guard the stores.

June 1. Rose at 6 a.m. All crews except ours were ready by 8.30 a.m. E.T.D. Skipper turned up at 8.55 and Mate 10 minutes later. Eventually got away at 9.30, towed behind the ketch " Heimat" by German M.L. B.6. The trip up the Schlei to Kappeln, near the mouth of the estuary, was very pleasant. Had sardine sandwich and char (tea) at 10 a.m. (char a bit cold). Being towed too fast, stern under most of the time, wallowing and pitching a bit, but nothing moved below decks.

Arrived Kiel (lock gates) at 4.30 after passing the Memorial and travelling up the estuary about two miles. Quite a number of sunken ships about, including some large vessels. Moved into lock at 5.25 p.m. The gates here slide across lock, unlike those seen in England. It was raining hard when we left Kiel at 6.30 p.m. We were towed up the canal at 8 knots and finally moored alongside some wooden piles at Landbergh.

Sunday, June 2. Had a spot of bother with the skipper over leaving two plates of partially eaten sausages in the cockpit while we went forward to make fast the towing rope. Let him have his say – anything for a quiet life. Got under way again at 9 a.m. Being towed too fast again and taking seas right into the cockpit at times. Skipper tried to hail towing M.L. with megaphone, but it was useless against the wind. Our skylight leaked badly, too, and our clothes and bedding below were soaked.

Arrived Brunsbuttel 4 o'clock and left again at 5 p. m.; heavy squalls made the three-mile tow across the Elbe estuary cold and wet, and we were glad to reach Cuxhaven at 7 p.m. More bad weather kept us at Cuxhaven for a fortnight, so carried out many odd jobs on boat.

June 12. Skipper of yacht " Sperling" (one of the other craft of the fleet) challenged us to a race around the Elbe 3 lightship during the afternoon. We were towed out of harbour (there is a rule that all vessels must be towed out) and had a bit of trouble getting jib set, but once started everything went wizard. We dead-beat to the Elbe light with the tide in our favour. On the return leg we set the Genoa and went inshore to miss the current. Took bearings and sounded constantly, but hit the mud just where clear water was shown on our chart. Fortunately the tide carried us off without doing any damage and the skipper signalled for the launch to tow us back. This was just as well perhaps, because there was a strong tide against us.

June 14. A hell of a night, wind gale force. At midnight we were awakened by Flt. Lt. Kenny, the organiser of the trip, who showed us how to fit the springs satisfactorily to ease the pounding against the pontoon. The yacht rode out the gale and the weather cleared a little during the day.

Sunday, June 16. Weather quite calm and received orders to get under way, although we did not actually get started until 5.15 in the afternoon. The sea was dead calm, but the speed at which we were being towed put our stern under water.

June 17. Night was wet and cold with slight sea running. We had nothing to eat since leaving Cuxhaven except bully beef sandwiches, because it was too rough to light the Primus stove. Sighted first of the Frisian Isles at 9 p.m. Sea got much rougher during the night, and we were all soaked. Eventually we just stripped off some of our wet clothes and turned in in our bunks. Tiffin time we tried to go alongside the M.L. for a meal, but bashed a hole in her stern with our stem, and we gave up the attempt. Had a slight disagreement with the skipper; he wanted Irish stew for lunch and we wanted sausages. We all had Irish stew!

The weather became too rough to continue, so we were towed towards Den Helder, one of the islands guarding the Zuider Zee. In reply to our inquiry, the M.L. signalled that this would take two hours; actually four hours passed before we were moored. With the violent motion, it was impossible to stay on our berths with the backs in position, so dumped them on the floor for use as duck boards as there was about 2 ins. of water swilling about. Eventually we were moored and started getting cleaned up while the skipper and mate went off to fix some grub. Den Helder was quite a pleasant spot, a fishing village, with many small yachts in the harbour. We changed a tin of tobacco for 10 guilders, and with the proceeds went to the nearest pub and supped stout.

June 18. Had breakfast on board the M.L. and got under way after fixing a few of the necessary odd jobs. Finally we got clear of the harbour, but struck a confused sea outside, which got steadily worse. But for the fact that it was only a short passage to our next port at Ijmniden, we would have turned back. We were pressing into a very strong south-westerly breeze, and took six hours to make the passage, taking on board more water in that time than we had in the whole 24 hours coming from Cuxhaven.

June 19. Spent the morning in cleaning up the ship, and decided later to go into Amsterdam. Had to panic to get the train, and finally arrived there at 7 p.m. Went across to the Victory Hotel for dinner after changing 20 cigarettes to pay for it. Met the skipper and mate on the way back, and on board we shared a tin of ham and-egg pie – all very pally.

June 20. The M.L. went outside the harbour to investigate the weather, and, as a result, it was decided that we were to stay until the weather eased. Went to Amsterdam later in the day.

June 21. Owing to a misunderstanding, the launches had to leave with only one yacht apiece. As our M.L. had been towing two boats, we were left behind to make our way to England as best we could.

June 22. Preparatory to setting sail for Blighty, the navigator had arranged for a Dutch tug to tow us clear of the harbour. The tug took us into the buoyed channel to set our sails and then left us to our own devices. We set our storm rig, and this was quite enough, and for the first time the wind was with us, north to north-west. The original intention was to put into the Hook of Holland, but to take advantage of the favourable wind it was decided to push on through the night.

Sunday, June 23. At 2 a.m. we were seven miles off Ostend, but by the time we reached the harbour entrance it was almost dead calm and we only just made it. Berthed alongside Navy buoy layers at 7.45 a.m. We had intended laying off the Royal Belgian Yacht Club, but the tide having set against us we could not make it.

June 24. At 7 a.m. we slipped our moorings, and with a light breeze and the tide with us had no difficulty in getting clear of the harbour. Once clear of the harbour we made for the buoy at the junction of the Flushing and Hook route, but we had quite a bit of difficulty in finding the mark, as there were loads of fishing smacks around, and the tide was now setting us in the opposite direction to that indicated on the chart. The wind was freshening all the time, and we sailed as close as we could. By 2.30 it had freshened too much and we had to take the Genoa off and set the storm jib. Later, it became squally, and it was necessary to take in a reef. After a while the wind eased a little, although it rained hard, and we shook out the reef again but left the storm jib on. We expected to sight Ramsgate at 9.30 p.m.

At about 5.15 it again became very squally and black, so we reefed down once more. There was quite a sea running, probably because of the shoals at the Goodwins, from which direction the wind was coming. Visibility became so bad that it was impossible to pick out the next buoy, and we sighted nothing more until 9.30 p.m., when we picked up the N. Foreland light, miles north of where we should have been. By this time the wind had dropped a lot, although there was quite a swell running, and with the tide against us we made little progress.

June 25. We passed the North Goodwin light vessel at 3.30 a.m., and at 6.30 we entered Ramsgate harbour and moored alongside the mole. Left Ramsgate at 2.30 p.m. With the storm jib set and working mainsail reefed down, tacked out of harbour. Once outside we set the working jib and shook out the reef. 3.30 p.m. found us aground to the south-west of the harbour entrance. We refloated at 4.30 and had just gained steerage way when the Ramsgate lifeboat came alongside and asked if we required assistance. Told them no and pressed on. We dead beat to the South Foreland with the lifeboat in attendance all the while. Finally, they left us, and a long-range R.A.F. launch sped out to see if we were o.k. Assured him that we were, and said we were making for Folkestone.

7.30 p.m. Wind dropped a mile from Dover Harbour. The current set us back, and after trying the sweeps which proved useless, made for St. Margaret's Bay and dropped anchor in five fathoms of water. Weighed anchor at 9.30 p.m. as wind seemed to have freshened, but moment anchor was aboard wind dropped. Tried beating against tide with wind S.S.W.

June 26. There was drizzling rain throughout the night and we started hourly watches. At 4.00 a.m. the " Pirol" was off Dover harbour. The tide carried us past the eastern entrance, and it was touch and go whether we should hit a wreck in the centre of the western approach, but the wind picked up at the critical moment and we just missed it. At 6.30 a.m. we berthed alongside the pilot boat, and turned in for three hours.

On awakening, we were told that we had been the cause of a great panic, and Coastal Command had sent a boat over to Belgium and Holland looking for us. The boat was then back in Dover Harbour before returning to base at Calshot, and intended taking us in tow. Too bad, that we could not finish the voyage under sail, but as there was a strong westerly wind still blowing perhaps it was just as well. We left Dover at noon, but wind freshened all the afternoon and forced us into Newhaven for the night.

June 27. Leaving Newhaven at 7.30 a.m., we pressed on to Calshot, arriving at 3.30 p.m. So the " Pirol" was home and we cleaned up and packed our kitbags. On talking the matter over with the other blokes, we learned that we were the last yacht to arrive. The others had followed the inland waterways from Den Helder to Flushing and had put into Calshot two days before we had made Dover.

It is a sad reminder of the passage of time that in the excellent displays to be seen in the Sunderland Hangar at Calshot and Calshot Castle today, including many photographs from 1917 to the present day, not one single reference is made to the Windfall yachts.

APPENDIX 12
PASSAGE OF THE 50 SQ M WINDFALL
SEESTURM to UK in AUGUST 1946

The next (abbreviated) account by cadet Wynne Edwards was written for the Christmas Term 1946 Britannia Royal Naval College Magazine. Permission to reproduce it is gratefully acknowledged. Wynne Edwards was a crew member of the 50 sq m SEESTURM (subsequently HAWK), skippered by his father.

OPERATION HOMEWARD V. *Being the journal of a voyage to Germany and Denmark and the bringing home of the 50 square metre German yacht "SEESTURM" across the North Sea to England.*

We sailed for Germany on August 4th bound for Kiel, in the destroyer "CYGNET." On board were about 40 other Officers and men, who were also taking part in Operation Homeward V, bringing home of German yachts as part of the reparations. Forty extra people in a destroyer is no small proposition, but this problem was solved by clearing the forward mess-deck which was to be our living quarters. I had quite a bit of fun slinging my hammock, and the whole of the first night was in peril of falling from it.

All next day we steamed up the swept channel about ten miles off the Dutch coast; even now, eighteen months after VE day, a large number of mines are still unswept, and it is necessary for ships to use channels which are swept regularly. These channels are marked with buoys at 25 mile intervals, thereby making navigation much easier. "CYGNET" was making for Wilhelmshaven, for here we were to disembark crews for two of the fifty square metre yachts which were lying here. Tuesday morning dawned, and on arriving on deck I found that we were lying at anchor in a thick mist. The party who were to land had been waiting on the cold and wet deck since 0330, having been told that this was our E.T.A., but owing to the mist we had been forced to anchor about a mile below Wilhelmshaven.

By 0900 we could make out details of the land, which was about a mile away on our starboard side – I was not very impressed by my first views of Germany – a gloomy, slightly rolling country-side, nearly bare of trees, and with not a sign of life anywhere. We could not see Wilhelmshaven but we could make out a large concrete building that appeared to have been a U-boat shelter.

As soon as possible we landed our crews and proceeded on our way. By 1430 we were steaming up the broad Elbe estuary, about 20 miles wide here and soon Cuxhaven hove in sight. We got into touch with the Naval base here by flashing at the mouth of the Kiel Canal, some 18 miles further up the estuary. I was much impressed by the size of the canal; it is wide enough for the largest ships and two ten thousand-tonners can pass each other quite comfortably.

We picked up a pilot at Brunnesbuttel, who was to take us through the canal. He was very strict about our not exceeding the speed limit and spotted it immediately when we increased to 10 knots. We had hoped previously to reach Kiel by dusk, but this soon appeared impossible, and we did not arrive in Kiel bay until very late that night.

Next morning as soon as possible we got our gear together and made for the jetty where the British Naval Base ship was lying. This was an exGerman liner, built by Blohm & Voss for the Turks in 1942; but when lying finished bombed and set on fire. Her stern is missing but otherwise she is completed. We were told that our yachts were still on the slipway on the other side of Kiel bay, so we dumped our gear in our respective cabins (which, incidentally, were the last word in luxury) and pushed off to have a look at the boats.

Lying on the slips in the ship-yard their lines impressed us very much – they were stoutly built and had been looked after well. The German builder who was responsible for their conditioning told us that ours would be ready in a week; this was a surprise for we had hoped to sail inside two days of our arrival; so, after some argument, we managed to persuade him we had to have our boat by Friday at the latest.

Next day, myself and one of crew, Lieut. van Win, a Dutch Naval Officer, set off in an Army car to cross the border to Denmark and get as much butter and eggs as possible. I will remember the road of Schleswig Holstein for a long time, for driving over cobbled roads for fifty miles or so, in a truck with no springs worth speaking of, is anything but comfortable. We reached the frontier about 1600, and after the usual formalities, crossed over into Denmark. The change was remarkable; no longer did we have those accursed cobbled roads. I was tremendously impressed by the tidiness of the countryside; the houses were all of red and white stone and looked very smart. After travelling about 30 miles we got to the small town of Aabenraa, and here we stopped. We had brought over with us several thousand cigarettes with which to barter, and these stood us in good stead. My only regret of that hectic hours' buying was that we hadn't enough cigarettes and money. We purchased altogether about 80 dozen eggs!

On Friday my Dutch friend and myself set out again, this time to see Kiel. We were both amazed by the damage; it really is incredible. You pass through mile after mile of streets, with only gaunt staring shells of homes to tell that here was a town. I just do not know how the Germans live in such a hell. The naval dockyard is battered into obliteration, and the whole scene is one of wholesale destruction.

I was very keen to get hold of a dachshund for my mother and I opened negotiations with the German who drove us round Kiel in a Volkswagen, These were not very successful. When I met him in the evening he apologised, and with tears in his eves exclaimed how difficult it was, but by tomorrow perhaps – we sailed at daybreak!

On Friday our yacht was ready: the "SEESTURM" (now here), as she was named, looked in perfect condition. Our only fear was for her sails, which looked none too new. That afternoon we had a sail drill in Kiel bay to get accustomed to sailing her; and all evening loaded up with stores for our long sea trip. Our crew was really perfect, and it would have been difficult to find a better. Besides my father and myself we had Lieut. Banbury, R.N.V.R., Dutchie (Lieut. R. Van win) and C.P.O. Merryweather.

By Saturday morning all was ready, and early on this day we were taken in tow by a German tug to begin the first stage of our journey. All that day we were towed through the Kiel canal, and we had an opportunity of testing our gear. The cooking was done with two primus stoves and was entrusted to Chief; we had arranged to form two watches: my father and myself in one, Banbury and Van Win in the other. Chief was to be spare and if wanted could help at any time. We tried the log out in the canal, but after much chartwork and calculation I found it had a big error; and owing to its size caused quite a drag on the boat. All the same it was useful, for it gave a rough estimation of our speed.

We didn't reach the end of the canal until it was getting dark. The tug was taking us on to Cuxhaven, which lies about 18 miles further down, but as there was a strong wind and tide against us, we decided to set sail and give the tug, which was a bit on the ancient side, a chance. When I turned in about 2230, the motion was getting quite violent and the prospect of getting to Cuxhaven seemed remote that night. I awoke to the sound of much noise on deck; sleepily I climbed out into the cockpit – it was pitch dark and blowing a full gale and the utmost confusion reigned. It appeared we had arrived at Cuxhaven, but nobody seemed to know where we were. I tottered back to my bunk feeling very tired. I was awakened early next morning by the sound of "Chief" singing his heart out and scrubbing the deck down – crawling out of my bunk I could see a blue sky overhead with white clouds soaring across it.

After breakfast my father and I went ashore to explore; the whole place appeared deserted, but at last we found a rather dirty old building, and here enquired where we could find the Naval Officer in Command – they didn't know but they had a telephone and after about twenty minutes we managed to find out the gen. It turned out that N.O.I.C. knew my father, and before long we were whisked off to his office – we both felt pretty dirty, and we were dressed in dirty old yachting clothes but the Captain of the base was kindness itself. He would not hear of us sailing that day, besides, he said, it was blowing a full gale out at Borkum and the Elbe light vessel. No, we must be his guests. The whole of that day we spent at his house, he had a beautiful garden and we just ate and slept: the food was absolutely wonderful with venison in lashings.

By 1800 the gale had blown itself out, so my father decided to risk it and sail that night. The weather forecast was good, and there was every prospect of fine weather. We were taken in tow out to the Elbe light vessel, for the mouth of the Elbe is tortuous with its many sand banks, and there was a strong tide. At midnight we reached our objective, and with a wish of good-cheer we parted our tow and set sail. It was a lovely night with a heavy ground swell running after the storm. The wind was light from the S.E. – altogether very pleasant.

Next day towards midday the wind died off and left us very nearly becalmed, the glass began to drop quickly, and we all sensed another spell of dirty weather. We were now off the westernmost of the Frisian islands, but there was no port we could possibly make without very intimate knowledge of the shoals, until Ijmuiden. We had no alternative but to go on and hope it wouldn't be too bad. By sunset (a watery one) we were pelting along, reaching, at about eight knots with our lee-rail under – it was a grand feeling. Supper was out of the question on the slanting table, so Chief gave it to us in cups – an excellent idea. I held the last dog watch and on being relieved at 2000 felt a pang of remorse, it was a grand feeling being at the tiller then.

I woke up from an uneasy sleep at midnight. The motion was now very rough, and I heard someone yelling to get " all hands on deck – I struggled up to the now madly pitching cockpit, and looked around me. It was pitch dark, but vaguely I could make out the forms of huge waves sweeping past on either side of us. The mainsail had torn with two reefs in it, and it was a job to lash it up to the boom to avoid it tearing more. The rather flimsy Genoa had to be taken in, too; and we put on a smaller foresail.

Back down below, but not to sleep. The motion was too violent, and one had to exert an effort to keep oneself in the bunk; besides, sea water dripped steadily on to my face from a crack in the roof. After hours the dawn broke; looking out of the tiny porthole I could see enormous seas towering high above us – it was a terrifying and inspiring sight. The cabin was the most terrible shambles, water was everywhere; for each person who came down below, took water with him. Food was impossible, so I dismally chewed biscuits and chocolate. The movement of the little boat was frightening by now, and I was beginning to wonder how much longer she would stand it – it certainly stands to the credit of the builders for she took a terrific hammering from the elements. Taking the tiller was absolutely hell; sea water cascaded in tons over the whole boat and swept down on one; the boat had to be kept head-on to the huge seas as far as it was possible to.

About mid-day the wind dropped suddenly, and inside two minutes sprang up with equal force from the North-west causing very steep and choppy seas; some of the waves being in the order of 30 feet from trough to crest, and very precipitous. About half-past one our foresail tore right across. There was nothing but to change it for our last sail, a small storm sail. This proved a tricky business owing to the furiously lashing foresheets that threatened to knock the wind out of one. Poor Chief got a terrific blow on his stomach from one of them that all but sent him overboard. The storm jib hoisted we ran for the land again, making an estimated five knots. With the steep seas, one experienced the thrill of surf-riding on a grand scale, and at times the ship surged forward at about 15 knots for a 100 yards or more on the slope of an on-coming wave. We were only pooped once when the cockpit was half-filled; we were ready for that, and quickly had it dry again. It certainly was a wonderful sensation running like we were.

At about 2100 land was sighted, and this turned out to be none other than Ijmuiden, by a marvellous piece of luck we had struck the only place on the coast where we could have found shelter. We secured alongside a Dutch L.C.T. whose crew were really wonderful to us. They dried our clothes, and gave us a huge great meal. I flopped into bed in my clothes, too tired to take them off. Next day we set about putting the boat in order, it was a terrible mess inside; in the afternoon, my father, Dutchie and myself set off for Amsterdam with our torn and tattered sails to get them repaired. The whole crew went to Amsterdam the next day by train to see the sights and do shopping. I had my hair cut for the fabulous price of 10/- but got a wonderful meal for 5/-. We returned back on board, having spent all our money and cigarettes, feeling very satisfied. The sailmaker made a very good job of the sails, but told us that the canvas was rotten – this we found to our cost later.

Crack of dawn Friday found us once more on our way – this time it seemed we were to be becalmed, and for a whole day we lay in placid water with a blazing sun, a pleasant change. The water was deliciously cool and we bathed in it. Two porpoises frolicked round us for a time, cruising just below the water like sharks and dashing with tremendous speed from place to place. In the evening a fresh easterly wind arose, and by 2200 had risen sufficiently to decide to furl the mainsail once more; we did not want to take any more risks. This we did, but misfortune again dogged us, for in the darkness and with the motion of the ship the sail got caught on some snag, whilst being stowed on deck, and ripped once more along some five feet of canvas. All night we made good progress, however, with an easterly wind, under a storm jib alone.

Next day, Chief and my father set about mending the mainsail with pillowcases – but owing to the rottenness of the sail, sailmaker's needles were useless, and we could only use darning needles and cotton. Before repairs were completed, and at about mid-day on Saturday, when approximately half-way between Dunkirk and Ramsgate, the wind veered rapidly through South and West to North and rose with amazing rapidity to gale force once more. Visibility shut down to about two miles, and in a short time high seas were again running, and went North, rising with amazing rapidity to gale force once more.

We had intended to make Dover that evening but under only one sail and a N.W. wind it was impossible to make certain of clearing the dreaded Goodwins and also to make the port; we therefore steered well to the Southward. When we did sight land it was clear we had been swept well to the south of Dover. The gale blew itself out towards evening, and by the light of a torch we completed repairs on the sails. I will always remember that night-sail down the Channel – it was a calm moonlight night, and the sea and wind had subsided. We held a sing-song on the deck, and fairly roared away; any ship passing us might have got the wrong impression – but we didn't care.

Next morning we rounded Selsey Bill, our faithful pillow-cases holding us good; and entered Chichester harbour, where we had decided to put in before entering Portsmouth. It had been a pretty tough fight – I had learnt a lot, and not least amongst this was the fury of the elements and what they could do. Yes, it was a wonderful experience.

"SEESTURM" had lived up to her name, but she had behaved magnificently. One last word for the crew: how lucky we were. I only hope I can meet them all again and renew old times.

C. J. C. WYNNE EDWARDS.

APPENDIX 13
THE NEAR LOSS OF THE 50 SQ M NORBEC
(LEOPARD) ON PASSAGE TO UK IN JULY 1946

This is an extract from an article "Gathering another Windfall" by Lt Cdr P J Fryer RNVR graphically describing his experience in the 50 sq m NORBEC during OPERATION HOMEWARD "where we encountered the worst storm at sea that I have ever experienced in my subsequent 40 years cruising". It is reproduced in part with grateful thanks to the RNSA, in whose journal the first full article was published.

On the 16 July 1946 I was one of some 40 volunteers who had answered the Admiralty's call. We embarked aboard HMS COMUS for Kiel with no idea of the type of yachts we were to sail back until an early briefing informed us that there were two 100 sq m and seven 50 sq m.

By the time we reached Kiel my namesake, Cdr Fryer, who was in charge of the flight, had allocated the crews and I found myself with Lt Crossley RN as Skipper and with Sub Lt Ireland RNVR – a South African and Midshipman Fforde, the son of the headmaster of Rugby School, making up the crew. It was late evening when we arrived at Kiel and were met by Cdr Martin Sherwood RN who was in charge of the German yachts. He was an experienced yachtsman who prior to the war had sailed "Tai-mo-Shan" from Singapore to Dartmouth with Capt Ryder (later VC) and other naval officers. He allocated us to NORBEC, one of the 50 sq m. Their Lordships had issued no instructions beyond stating that the yachts were to be delivered safe and sound to Portsmouth.

The yachts generally were in poor condition. In NORBEC we had no large scale charts, no wireless, no barometer, no spare ropes or tackle and of course, no electronic navigation aids: nor were the yachts equipped with guard-rails. Commander Sherwood thought we ought to have a shake down cruise before setting off for Portsmouth and organised a 60 mile race across the Baltic to Rodby Havn, a small fishing village on the island of Laaland, in which all the yachts took part including the two 100 sq m ROBBE and MARABU.

The outward trip was uneventful with light winds and a calm sea but we did have some difficulty with the mainsail slides when hoisting and lowering the sail. In harbour the following morning we found a strong wind blowing straight into the narrow harbour entrance. As a result the general decision was that it would be impossible to beat out. I had just returned from a family holiday sailing the narrow waters of the Norfolk Broads and felt certain there would be no difficulty. The 50 sq m can turn in its own length and is quick on the helm – so after some discussion

I persuaded Crossley to let me take her out. This we did successfully and the rest of the yachts then followed us out.

Outside the harbour we soon found NORBEC to be a very wet ship – added to which she was leaking badly, requiring frequent pumping. Late in the afternoon our main sail split from luff to leach and we had to take in a couple of reefs to cover the split. Shortly afterwards the after port shroud parted to be followed a little later by the starboard shroud. We were still 15 miles from Kiel when we were taken in tow by a German tug which already had another of the 50 sq m in tow. The race back from Rodby Havn was won by Lt Scott RNVR in SEEOTTER (it was actually ZEISIG) – a creditable performance as he had no chart of the Baltic and a faulty compass. The only other yacht to finish was manned by four submariners.

There was plenty to do on our return to Kiel as the race had disclosed numerous defects in nearly all the yachts. The riggers came aboard NORBEC and removed all our standing rigging, while we tried in vain to get a replacement for our mainsail which was rotten. According to my log it split seven times on our trip to Portsmouth. We were equally unsuccessful in getting a trysail, a wireless or a barometer.

On 24 July at 0700 we finally slipped our moorings and together with SEEFALKE, another 50 sq m, were taken by tug through the Kiel Canal. This gave us an opportunity to correct what charts we had which were badly out of date. It was early evening when we arrived at Brunsbruttal – dropped our tow – hoisted sail and crossed the Elbe to Cuxhaven. HMS FARNDALE was in port and they stocked us with "duty free" and gave us a weather report which was not an encouraging one.

The following morning was dull and wet but we were anxious to make a start and left Cuxhaven at 0900 in a light breeze from the South West. In the afternoon the weather cleared and the sun broke through. The evening developed into a beautiful clear starry night, the wind fell away and the sea became like glass. At 2200 we sighted the lights of Nordeney – we were then becalmed for several hours but by midday we had the Oster EMS buoy abeam. The wind then backed to ESE and with a fair wind we decided to carry on as far as Ijmuiden and there enter the North Sea Canal. It was a glorious day with not a cloud in the sky – but for some reason I got an uneasy feeling that the weather was going to change and that we were in for a "blow". We had taken the precaution of studying our small scale chart for possible bolt holes, as in the event of a gale, we were worried about the condition of our mainsail and standing rigging – mostly "ersatz" rope. The most likely bolt holes seemed to be behind the Eastern end of Terschelling or behind Vlieland or, possibly, Texel.

We continued to make steady progress in the light East South Easterly wind until 1920 when the wind, very suddenly, veered to the South West and increased in strength. This caught us in an involuntary gybe which resulted in a broken port crosstree. The sea rapidly lost its calm and within half an hour we were running before a big following sea – although there was no weight in the wind. At our present rate of progress we estimated that we should be off the Texel at around midnight and we'd slip into Den Helder. The wind continued to increase and then came a sudden and quite terrific thunderstorm with lightening flashing all around us for over an hour. We seemed to be in the centre of the storm and it was quite frightening. It became necessary to reef as the mainsail was beginning to split. This proved difficult because the sail was soaking wet and it was almost impossible to remove the lower sail batten. We could see the lights of Terschelling and for a moment considered running in behind the island for shelter – but further examination of the chart was sufficient to deter us in the existing weather conditions, which were deteriorating all the time. We decided to carry on to Texel some 28 miles further on.

It seemed essential that when we reached Texel around midnight one of us should be sufficiently fresh to take her into the harbour. I slept soundly in spite of the noise until just after midnight when I came on deck to be met by the most appalling conditions. The wind during my watch below had again veered to the South West and the seas were mountainous and breaking. I was surprised to see that we were heading 350° – our mainsail was once again splitting and it was essential to reduce sail further. We found it quite impossible to bring NORBEC head to wind but we did manage to take down the foresail.

The Skipper and crew had now been on deck for several hours but declined to go below for a spell. I managed to produce four cups of hot cocoa on an old primus which was not in gimbals and consequently had to be balanced on the cabin floor. With the weather continuing to deteriorate the Skipper decided we must get down the mainsail and run under bare poles – the mast was whipping like a fishing rod owing to the loss of the shroud. We attached a rope to the Skipper and for over an hour struggled to get the mainsail down and stowed – the mast had developed a twist which caused the slides to jam. He eventually succeeded but got a bad knock on the head from a foresheet block. While all this was happening we lost the rotator from the log and we had no spare. To add to our difficulties we were pooped on several occasions and we made another attempt to bring her head to sea with a sea anchor over the bows. This was a mistake – we should have streamed it over the stern. Assembling the sea anchor involved crawling into the fo'castle which was in a shambles. Masses of ropes, blocks, sails and sailbags and gear of all kind had come adrift over which a gallon of paraffin had been spilt.

We had pinned great hopes on the sea anchor but when we heaved it over the bows and slowly paid out 40 fathoms of 3 inch warp the only effect was to pull NORBEC's head round by some 45° so that we were now nearly beam on to the breaking seas. It was essential to get in the sea anchor – but this proved impossible with the warp bar taut – so we had to cut it adrift. By 0300 it had been blowing between Force 8–9, with gusts of Force 10, for several hours. The seas were mountainous, rushing up on our port quarter we were lifted up and then rode down the backs of them with a mighty crash as we hit the trough. At intervals a sea would break over us – we were all beginning to feel the strain. Crossley after his fight with the mainsail and the knock on the head was exhausted and in some pain. Ireland had been at the helm for several hours and insisted in carrying on as he said that it gave him something to do. Fforde, in spite of considerable sea sickness was cheerful and optimistic and was a wonderful member of the crew throughout the trip. As the oldest member of the crew I felt it was up to me to do something – but I had never been caught out in conditions that even approached the present gale and did not know what further action we could take. We had a self-draining cockpit, now full of water, should we lash the helm, batten down the hatches and stay below until the weather eased? We were heading North and the nearest land a few hundred miles to leeward. Or should someone stay on deck in case of a serious emergency?

It was now 0345. I looked below where Crossley and Fforde were on their bunks. The floor boards were awash and there was a bottle of whisky floating around. We had begun to ship solid seas with greater frequency and when I found myself trying to bail out the cockpit with a tea cup (!) I realised I was beginning to suffer from fatigue. Fford got up and manned the bilge pump – but it could not cope and we seemed to be shipping water faster than we couldn't pump it out. We tried buckets but it made little difference.

It was at this point that I became convinced we were not going to survive. The storm was increasing all the time and the seas getting bigger and we were being blinded with spray which was lashing like a whip. The extraordinary thing was that with this conviction all trace of fear left me. Some part of me seemed to become detached and become an onlooker. Some years later reading Hilaire Belloc's "Cruise of the Nona" I discovered that he had had a similar experience when caught in a Force 10 gale in "Bardsey Sound". He wrote: "I discovered myself to be for the first time in my life entirely indifferent of my fate . . . in the grip of a tremendous gale and an angry countering sea yet I could only look with indifference on the sea and the land. It had no relation to courage". The fear came later.

I was aroused from this mental state when suddenly I thought I saw the port and starboard navigation lights of an approaching vessel. I called the others but they were convinced I was beginning to suffer from delusions. We were, after all, miles out of the swept channel and it was unlikely there would be any shipping in this unswept area – and Ireland, at the helm, had seen nothing. Crossley and Fforde were about to return below when the lights again appeared and this time we all saw them. Crossley disappeared below, reappearing with the rocket pistol and fired four flares. Firing the flares had the effect of bringing me back to the realisation of the seriousness of our position – and it was then I experienced fear.

We continued firing rockets at intervals until we eventually saw an answering flare but the vessel seemed to be getting no closer. About an hour after the first sighting the navigation lights the bows of a fishing trawler loomed out of the darkness. She cut across our bows and attempted to pass a line down wind – but was unsuccessful. She then rounded up some 150–200 yards to windward and floated a buoy down to us to which was attached a heaving line. We managed to retrieve the buoy and hauled in the line to which were attached two 3 inch warps. We made both fast and slowly the trawler steamed ahead paying out many fathoms of warp. She seemed to be about a quarter of a mile ahead before we felt the first strain . . . but within minutes both warps had parted!

The trawler came round again and made several attempts to get another line *aboard by the same method – but were unsuccessful. She then made a wide circle cutting across our bows (we were still making 5 knots under bare poles) and with inches to spare, so close in fact that they were able to hand me, on the foredeck, a wire hawser. It was a wonderful piece of seamanship on their part with us within inches of a collision. Meanwhile the trawler was steaming away quite fast to avoid our colliding with her. The only thing I could do was to take several turns round the mast with the hawser, to give a "spring" effect, and then bend a rope onto the eye splice and take this to one of the sheet winches. But I expected the wire to cut through the mast and bring it down.*

The trawler then returned and offered to take us aboard, but this was declined as it seemed impossible in the existing conditions. The trawler then commenced the tow on a very long hawser – in fact we only caught occasional glimpses of her stern light when each of us was on top of a sea. NORBEC rode reasonably well at first but the seas continued to build up and periodically the tow would lighten just when we were halfway up a wave and we would be pulled through it with the yacht completely submerged. Pumping and buckets had little effect. The strain on the wire hawser was terrific and we began to roll badly. Then the water in the cabin began to rise more quickly and we discovered that we were now shipping water through a cut in the bows – the wire had begun to cut through topsides and deck.

At 0640 we decided we would have to abandon ship before she sank under us – so we sent up more flares. The trawler stopped and rounded up to windward and then allowed herself to drift down on us – broadside on. We decided it would have to be each man for himself. We had discussed taking to the rubber dinghy, fearing NORBEC's topsides would be stove in when the trawler came alongside – but this plan we abandoned. As the trawler drifted down on us we were both rolling badly. We met with a terrific crash – but with the trawler's topsides 15–20 ft above us there was no chance of any of us getting aboard. We drifted apart to come together again with another almighty crash. This time Ireland made a big leap and managed to grab the bulwarks and there he hung as we drifted apart again. Seeing the danger of Ireland being crushed in our next impact two of the crew reached over, caught him by his pants and literally flung him onto the deck just in time. He landed on his head and was slightly concussed. The next time we crashed the trawler's topsides were below the level of Norbeck's deck and all we had to do was step aboard as easily as stepping onto a moving staircase! Once aboard the trawler, "De Jonge Jochem–DH8" kept NORBEC in tow and lightened by the absence of her four-man crew she rode higher in the water and remained in tow until we reached Den Helder. We were all forcibly put to bed with a large dose of Schnapps and there we slept until we arrived at Den Helder at 1130. The whole rescue was a marvellous exhibition of seamanship by the trawler's Skipper, Capt Post. The question of salvage was brushed aside by the Skipper who told us that he himself had been rescued by a British destroyer during the war.

We were invited to stay at the RNN establishment while NORBEC under-went a refit. We spent Sunday 28 July assessing the damage – planks in the hull required renewing – sails needed major repairs and all standing rigging had to be replaced. So for the next week we were in the hands of shipwrights, riggers, sailmakers and the Pilot (Harbour Master) and many others all of whom worked like trojans and showed us extraordinary hospitality. Each evening we were invited to the home of one or other of the craftsmen working on NORBEC.

On Saturday 3 August we threw a farewell party aboard NORBEC for all who had been so hospitable and early on the following morning we left our berth with our friend "The Pilot" who set us on our way to Ijmuiden via the North Holland Canal. The rest of the voyage was full of interest – but that is another story. We were joined in Amsterdam by Scott in SEEOTTER (actually ZEISIG) and sailed through the canals to Rotterdam – fetching up at the Yacht Club.

We continued through the canals to Ijmuiden where we left SEEOTTER (ZEISIG) and the canals and took to the sea. We visited Ostend and from there set sail for Portsmouth on the 18 August and we had a pleasant sail to Dover where we had to put in for repairs to the mainsail. Twice more we had to stop for the same reason – first into Shoreham and then anchoring at Eastbourne. We finally reached Portsmouth at 2100 on Friday 23 August, just five weeks after setting out. NORBEC was allocated to BRNC Dartmouth and was renamed LEOPARD.

Finally reflecting on our North Sea experience I endorse some words of Cdr Erroll Bruce to the effect that anyone who has endured a storm at sea from the cockpit of a small yacht could never complain that his life had been dull, even if nothing else had ever happened to him.

APPENDIX 14

PASSAGE OF THE 90 SQ M WINDFALL
BORKUM TO UK. SEPTEMBER 1946

The following account of acquiring BORKUM, subsequently renamed CAPELLA, was written early in 1947, then later in the RNSA Journal. She was in the last of eight batches of yachts in OPERATION HOMEWARD, sailing in September 1946. Clearly it was a fast and seamanlike passage despite the sails being in poor condition. It is reproduced here in part with grateful thanks to the RNSA.

GATHERING A WINDFALL by Capt John Wells CBE DSC RN

'*En route to UK from the Far East in August 1946 an Admiralty message was received on board my ship asking for volunteer yachtsmen to bring home the final group of ex-German naval yachts subsequently known as Windfalls. As a two and a half striper I sent in my name and sailed in a destroyer for Kiel late in September with a party of officers for OPERATION HOMEWARD. A warm welcome awaited us in Kiel in the shape of Cdr Martyn Sherwood, Senior Officer (Yachts) and a most entertaining personality.*

Next day we were taken to look at the boats where the spin of a coin made me skipper of BORKUM, a 90 sq m Bermudan sloop built for the German Navy in 1938 and laid up in Hamburg throughout the war. Although damaged in air raids BORKUM had been refitted with all the skill that was left in Kiel. And here she was looking a picture once more, her freshly varnished hull contrasting with the white sail cover secured neatly on the boom. Down below was a sparsely furnished saloon, after cabin with two bunks and a tiny galley with pressure stove. The auxiliary engine was an old four cylinder petrol model that had seen better days and only functioned spasmodically. My crew of five included an RN as well as an RNR lieutenant and two midshipmen RNVR who had, incidentally, never sailed before. Over the weekend we embarked stores and charts from the German Arsenal – "How many pairs of binoculars would you like, Sir?" – and two days later in company with MELBA, another 90 sq m, we sailed for a weekend shake down cruise.

In four hours the BORKUM was within Danish territorial waters, not far from the German port of Flensburg, and our eyes could pick out the little entrance to the town of Sonderburg to the NW. Rounding a beacon we entered a narrow channel and sailed into harbour under headsails.

Food in the Steamerhausen was excellent, there being an abundance of everything that was strictly rationed in England. With lager beer and a three-man orchestra playing all the old-fashioned tunes, time passed quickly. The next day we bought eggs, milk and butter for breakfast, then explored the town, admiring its clean, fresh appearance. The shop windows were full of British exports never seen in our country and it was a pleasure to see the flaxen-haired children running about with all the energy and happiness that comes from a well-fed nation.

In accordance with instructions we attempted to leave for Kiel the next day in a South- Westerly gale, taking the boats out in tow of a friendly motor launch, as both auxiliary engines were defective. Within minutes the midshipmen were seasick, the motor launch broke down before we were clear of the channel, and it was necessary to make several short tacks to clear the shallows. The mainsail let the side down by gradually tearing itself out of the runners on the mast track, the fault of ersatz seizing twine that on subsequent investigation proved little more than twisted paper. MELBA fared little better, and both boats were back in harbour by noon feeling a little ashamed at having to surrender to the elements. After refitting the mainsail we got down to the job of checking the running rigging, a certain amount of which had already shown signs of wear. BORKUM sailed at 1015 on the following forenoon, returning to Kiel at sunset after an uneventful passage.

It was the intention of the Senior Officer (Yachts) in MARABU to take the BORKUM and LADY EVE, leaving the MELBA to come home in a landing ship, much to the disappointment of her crew. The newcomers were both of similar size to ourselves and equally ready for sea. An anticyclone appeared to be hovering over the Azores, so we took the plunge and started off early one afternoon, each of the three yachts in tow of a German tug. No less than three pilots came on board in succession to see us safely through the Kiel Canal, allowing all hands to go below and prepare for what was to come. Meanwhile I had chosen the Lieutenant RN to be navigator, because he was Captain of an MTB and said he knew the coast. He turned out to be first-rate and worked as my oppo when we split up the company into two watches.

We got to Brunsbuttel at midnight to find the weather still favourable, still in tow, we pressed on together out of the mouth of the Elbe, past Cuxhaven and into the open sea, where BORKUM objected to being on the leash. Thirteen-ton yachts do not tow comfortably at more than slow speed and eventually the tug skipper condescended to reduce to 7 knots, muttering threats that were vaguely connected with the sooting up of diesels.

At 0930 we cast off the tow. Setting jib and staysail, BORKUM soon overhauled MARABU, under tow and ahead of us. The wind veered to the East (Force 3) and we found ourselves making over 7 knots in a following sea, which the boat rode with comfort. As a precautionary measure I took two reefs in the mainsail before dark in the event of having to tack next morning. More excitement occurred just after midnight. Whilst trying to pick up an unlit buoy the 2 knot current must have carried us well inshore, because we touched bottom on one of the many shallow patches off the Texel Island. It was an awkward moment. However, there was an off-shore wind and, altering course to seaward, we eventually picked up the line of buoys, finding one more unlit and another showing the wrong characteristics. The crew had little sleep that night. At 0630 I altered course at the entrance to Dan Helder and, rounding a buoy, the runner block in the starboard jib sheet parted its strop. Before it could be secured the broken pieces had torn the sail cloth severely.

Passing the LADY EVE, which had come up from the southward, we beat up very slowly against a strong ebb tide and – because of the sand banks – had to use the hand lead continually. But for the skipper of a passing garbage lighter, who sportingly volunteered to tow us into the lock, we should have taken some time to reach our haven that lay in a small pocket above the town. Our flagship had already made contact with the authorities, and two hours later all three yachts were under way in tow of a Dutch naval tug, leisurely making our way down the North Holland Ship Canal. It was a fine afternoon with the warm sun on the starboard beam, ripe for the drying of clothes and resting of bodies.

That night we secured at Pumerend, a few miles short of Amsterdam, pressing on the next morning to berth in Sixhaven, where the Yacht Club secretary made a point of meeting us within a few minutes of arrival. Unhappily the trail of war had spoilt all club facilities; but the Dutch Navy again came to the rescue, providing us with baths and much advice as to what to do in Amsterdam. That night it stood us in good stead.

The weather continued fine; and, on advice from the local met of office, I decided to press on, much to the chagrin of my crew whose supply of duty free cigarettes could buy virtually anything! There was little or no wind when we reached Imuiden, and yet I had a hunch we should get better luck outside. The engine was started and in some remarkable way was able to drive us clear of the harbour. Half an hour after midnight it gave up, never to start again. In silence the watch on deck hoisted sails, stuck a knife in the mast and whistled softly for the wind. Shortly after 0300 a breeze sprang up from the North East and by 0400 we were shaping a South-Westerly course at 4 knots. This progress was too much for the mainsail, which fell down at 0630, enveloping the helmsman. Visions of splicing a new halliard were dispelled when I saw the cause was due to the pawl of the winch drum, which had jumped out and fractured itself

We picked up a line of buoys which enabled us to shape a course down the main shipping lane and there was plenty of work for hands on deck, who scarcely noticed a big Swedish merchantman dip her flag to our miniature White Ensign. That act of courtesy gave us the biggest boost of the voyage. And so the day passed and darkness fell to find us looking warily for wreck buoys. By that time it was apparent that small craft are very much at the mercy of Channel tides and it was a relief to sight the glow of the East Goodwin light-vessel at midnight. From that moment all was plain sailing; and although the wind dropped occasionally it kept us moving sufficiently fast to make Dover at 0730. Proceeding steadily westwards, the rest of that final day and night was an anticlimax. Arriving off Portsmouth harbour we tacked for the first time since leaving Imuiden, the first tack of many before securing close to Asia Pontoon at 0300. Before turning in I reckoned that the BORKUM, with the RNSA burgee at the mast head, had sailed 500 miles in

84 hours at an average speed of just under 6 knots. It was hard to believe that our voyage was at an end.

On the following day we turned her over to CinC Portsmouth, and all hands packed up to go ashore, taking with them unshaven faces, dirty bodies, a few "rabbits" and perhaps a happy memory of the North Sea. We had learnt a good many lessons in seamanship, pilotage and cooking, met a number of diverse personalities in three foreign countries and acquired the ability to live comfortably together in confined quarters. Above all, we realised that the Navy had acquired magnificent opportunities for sail training since the end of 1947 every large shore establishment, including the RNVR divisions, will be possessors of first class sailing craft ranging from 30 to over 100 sq m in size. Not only will ocean racing circles benefit from these additions but it should be possible for almost any officer or rating to take advantage of the opportunities offered for cruising and racing around the coasts of the United Kingdom. Our BORKUM will soon be the property of the RNVR. May those who sail her have all the luck and adventure of her prize crew.

BORKUM was eventually handed over to Humber Division RNVR for some years and renamed CAPELLA. She was later returned to the RN where she was allocated firstly to HMS DRYAD and then to the Britannia Royal Naval College Dartmouth, remaining there until 1972.

APPENDIX 15. 1954 Survey of Admiralty Windfalls

Yacht	Establishment	Hull	Spars	Sails	Category
Seehexe	HMS Daedalus	Fair	Good	Fair	B
Sea Horse	RNB Portsmouth	Poor	Good	Fair	C
Meon Maid	HMS Mercury	Poor	Fair	Fair	B
Sea Feather	HMS Dolphin	Fair	Fair	Fair	A
Sea Otter	HMS Vernon	Fair	Good	Fair	A
Sea Wraith	HMS Excellent	Fair	Fair	Fair	B
Sea Soldier	RMB Eastney	Fair	Fair	Fair	B
Sea Scamp	RNB Plymouth	Good	Fair	Fair	A
Sea Swallow	HMS Defiance	Good	Fair	Good	A
Disdaine	RNB Plymouth	Poor	Fair	Poor	C
Wal	HMS Collingwood	Fair	Fair	Fair	B
Marabu	HMS Hornet	Good	Fair	Fair	A
Capella	HMS Dryad	Fair	Poor	Fair	B
Planet	HMS Fisgard	Poor	Poor	Poor	C
Sigrid	SORF Clyde	Poor	Fair	Fair	C
Nimrod	HMS Osprey	Fair	Fair	Fair	B
Korsar	HMS St Vincent	Poor	Poor	Fair	C
Jutta	RNB Chatham	Poor	Poor	Good	C

Notes:

1. The list only refers to Naval Windfalls and excludes the seven naval yachts (GRYPHIS, HAWK, MARTLET, HARPY, PEGASUS, LEOPARD and GALAHAD) at the Dartmouth and Plymouth Naval Colleges which were maintained at Admiralty expense and did not need a further independent survey.

2. The Categories are:
   A. Yachts which have a remaining life of 5 or more years.
   B. Those which may be expected to last three seasons.
   C. Those in poor condition and should be replaced.

Appendix 16: Windfalls in Fastnet Races

Year	Class	Yacht	Type	Representing	Position
1937		Asta	85 ft Yawl	Marine Regatta Verein	17/29
1939	1	Nordwind	60 ton Yawl	Kriegsmarine. Line honours	10/26
1947	1	Orion	150 sq m	RN Sailing Association	8/9
	2	Seamew	50 sq m	Royal Engineer YC	dnf
1949	1	Avalanche	100 sq m	Royal Engineer YC	4/9
	1	Helgoland	59 ft yawl	RNB Portsmouth	dnf
	2	Sea Otter	50 sq m	HMS Vernon	4/20
	2	Galahad	20 ton	RN Engineering College	dnf
	2	Sea Wraith	50 sq m	HMS Excellent	dnf
	2	Sea Feather	50 sq m	HMS Dolphin	dnf
	2	Leopard	50 sq m	BRNC Dartmouth	dnf
	2	Harpy	50 sq m	BRNC Dartmouth	dnf
1951	1	Marabu	100 sq m	HMS Hornet	5/13
	1	Kranich	100 sq m	Royal Air Force	8/13
	1	Overlord	100 sq m	Royal Engineer YC	9/13
	1	Aegir X	150 sq m	British Kiel YC	dnf
	1	Lively	125 sq m	British Kiel YC	dnf
1953	1	Marabu	100 sq m	HMS Hornet	8/12
	1	Overlord	100 sq m	Royal Engineer YC	11/12
	1	Nordwind	60 ton Yawl	H W Astor (private entry)	dnf
	2	Disdaine	50 sq m	HMS Drake	8/19
1955	1	Marabu	100 sq m	RNVR SC	8/12
	1	Gladeye	100 sq m	Household Brigade	9/12
	1	Flamingo	100 sq m	2nd TAF SC	12/12
	3	Planet	60 sq m	HMS Fisgard	13/22
1957	1	Marabu	100 sq m	HMS Hornet	dnf
	1	Overlord	100 sq m	RASC YC	dnf
	1	Gladeye	100 sq m	Household Brigade	dnf
	2	Disdaine	50 sq m	RN Barracks Devonport	dnf
	2	See Hexe	50 sq m	Home Air Command SC	dnf
1959	1	Marabu	100 sq m	C in C Portsmouth	11/15
	1	Capella	90 sq m	BRNC Dartmouth	dnf
	2	Sea Wraith	50 sq m	HMS Excellent	dnf
1961	1	Marabu	100 sq m	C in C Portsmouth	14/24
1963	1	Marabu	100 sq m	RN Coastal Forces SC	28/35
	1	Merlin	100 sq m	Home Air Command SC	23/35
1965	1	Marabu	100 sq m	C in C Portsmouth	29/33

ACRONYMS

ASA	Army Sailing Association
A & R	Abeking and Rasmussen
ASMY	Association for Square Metre Yachts
ASYC	Association of Service Yacht Clubs
ASMYC	Association of Square Metre Yacht Clubs
BAOR	British Army on the Rhine
BKYC	British Kiel Yacht Club
BM	Burmester
BRNC	Britannia Royal Naval College Dartmouth
C in C	Commander in Chief
DoT	Department of Trade
ECYC	European Classic Yacht Union
GKW	Gerdhardt Kroger Werft
HMS	Her Majesty's Ship
IALA	International Association of Lighthouse Authorities
LOA	Length Overall
LWL	Length Waterline
M & P	Mathieson & Paulsen
MRV	Marine-Regatta-Verein
OCC	Offshore Cruising Club
PGO	Portsmouth General Order
RACYC	Royal Armoured Corps Yacht Club
RAF	Royal Air Force
RAFYC	Royal Air Force Yacht Club
RAN	Royal Australian Navy
RASCYC	Royal Army Service Corps Yacht Club
RAYC	Royal Artillery Yacht Club
REYC	Royal Engineer Yacht Club
RLM	Reicsluftfahrtministerium (Reich Air Ministry)
RMA	Royal Military Academy Sandhurst
RMB	Royal Marine Barracks
RN	Royal Navy
RNB	Royal Navy Barracks
RNEC	Royal Naval Engineering College
RNSA	Royal Naval Sailing Association
RNVR	Royal Naval Volunteer Reserve
RNZN	Royal New Zealand Navy
RORC	Royal Ocean Racing Club
RSSA	Royal Signals Sailing Association
RYA	Royal Yachting Association
RYS	Royal Yacht Squadron
Sq M	Square Metre
SNOSH	Senior Naval Officer Schleswig Holstein

INDEX

Page numbers in bold type represent photographs.

The Author

Michael Cudmore joined the Royal Navy as a Cadet (E) in 1954 and served in various theatres world wide including the Falklands Campaign in which he was awarded the OBE. On leaving the service in 1986 as a Commander he went into the aviation industry for nine years followed by a period as a consultant.

Like most servicemen of his time he was introduced to offshore sailing in Windfalls. A regular offshore sailor for over forty years, he sailed principally in European waters and in 1998 crossed the Atlantic in a 28 foot Twister. He was Chairman of the RNSA Air Branch for five years, is a member of the Royal Ocean Racing Club and the Society for Nautical Research. He continues to sail and is involved with a number of local activities, principally connected with rural and maritime history. Married with two children he lives in Somerset.

FUTURE WINDFALL ARCHIVES

By its nature this book is incomplete and will expose areas that require further research. As more information comes to light there will be a need to have a central location for Windfall records.

The Bartlett Library at the National Maritime Museum Cornwall already has excellent archives and holds the National Small Boat Register (for all historic craft under 40 feet LOA which would include the 30 sq m Windfalls). 30 sq m Windfall owners are invited to register their craft on the NSBR. In addition the Library has kindly agreed to have a specific Windfall Register for the yachts over 40 feet, starting with the lists from this book. The contact details are: Bartlett Library, National Maritime Museum Cornwall, Discovery Quay, Falmouth TR11 3QY. library@nnmc.co.uk

Rear Cover:
Top.   Kiel Regatta 1936. 50 sq m *Seeotter* in the foreground
Bottom.   Seven 50 sq m Windfalls leaving Plymouth on the 1951 St Malo Race